How Serious a Problem Is Drug Use in Sports?

Hal Marcovitz

INCONTROVERSY

ReferencePoint
Press®

San Diego, CA

ReferencePoint Press®

About the Author

A former journalist, Hal Marcovitz is the author of more than 150 books for young readers. His other titles in the In Controversy series include *Should Juvenile Offenders Be Tried as Adults?* and *How Should America Respond to Illegal Immigration?*

For more information, contact:
ReferencePoint Press, Inc.
PO Box 27779
San Diego, CA 92198
www.ReferencePointPress.com

Picture credits:
Cover: iStockphoto.com
AP Images: 12, 19, 35, 46, 56, 65, 70
© Bettmann/Corbis: 7
Thinkstock/Image Source: 72
Thinkstock/iStockphoto: 40, 50, 77
© George Tiedemann/GT Images/Corbis: 29

LIBRARY OF CONGRESS CATALOGING-IN-PUBLICATION DATA

Marcovitz, Hal.
  How serious a problem is drug use in sports? / by Hal Marcovitz.
    p. cm. -- (In controversy)
  Includes bibliographical references and index.
  ISBN-13: 978-1-60152-448-5 (hardback)
  ISBN-10: 1-60152-448-X (hardback)
 1. Doping in sports--Juvenile literature. 2. Athletes--Drug use--Juvenile literature. I. Title.
  RC1230.M367   2013
  362.29--dc23

                                         2012005995

Contents

Foreword

In 2008, as the US economy and economies worldwide were falling into the worst recession since the Great Depression, most Americans had difficulty comprehending the complexity, magnitude, and scope of what was happening. As is often the case with a complex, controversial issue such as this historic global economic recession, looking at the problem as a whole can be overwhelming and often does not lead to understanding. One way to better comprehend such a large issue or event is to break it into smaller parts. The intricacies of global economic recession may be difficult to understand, but one can gain insight by instead beginning with an individual contributing factor, such as the real estate market. When examined through a narrower lens, complex issues become clearer and easier to evaluate.

This is the idea behind ReferencePoint Press's *In Controversy* series. The series examines the complex, controversial issues of the day by breaking them into smaller pieces. Rather than looking at the stem cell research debate as a whole, a title would examine an important aspect of the debate such as *Is Stem Cell Research Necessary?* or *Is Embryonic Stem Cell Research Ethical?* By studying the central issues of the debate individually, researchers gain a more solid and focused understanding of the topic as a whole.

Each book in the series provides a clear, insightful discussion of the issues, integrating facts and a variety of contrasting opinions for a solid, balanced perspective. Personal accounts and direct quotes from academic and professional experts, advocacy groups, politicians, and others enhance the narrative. Sidebars add depth to the discussion by expanding on important ideas and events. For quick reference, a list of key facts concludes every chapter. Source notes, an annotated organizations list, bibliography, and index provide student researchers with additional tools for papers and class discussion.

The *In Controversy* series also challenges students to think critically about issues, to improve their problem-solving skills, and to sharpen their ability to form educated opinions. As President Barack Obama stated in a March 2009 speech, success in the twenty-first century will not be measurable merely by students' ability to "fill in a bubble on a test but whether they possess 21st century skills like problem-solving and critical thinking and entrepreneurship and creativity." Those who possess these skills will have a strong foundation for whatever lies ahead.

No one can know for certain what sort of world awaits today's students. What we can assume, however, is that those who are inquisitive about a wide range of issues; open-minded to divergent views; aware of bias and opinion; and able to reason, reflect, and reconsider will be best prepared for the future. As the international development organization Oxfam notes, "Today's young people will grow up to be the citizens of the future: but what that future holds for them is uncertain. We can be quite confident, however, that they will be faced with decisions about a wide range of issues on which people have differing, contradictory views. If they are to develop as global citizens all young people should have the opportunity to engage with these controversial issues."

In Controversy helps today's students better prepare for tomorrow. An understanding of the complex issues that drive our world and the ability to think critically about them are essential components of contributing, competing, and succeeding in the twenty-first century.

The Steroid Era

For Randy Maris and Roger Maris Jr., the ceremony honoring their father at Yankee Stadium in New York was a bittersweet experience. It was September 24, 2011, the date the Yankees selected to commemorate the fiftieth anniversary of the sixty-first home run of the season slugged by the late Roger Maris. The Yankees outfielder hit the homer on October 1, 1961. Maris's homer is considered a tremendous feat because it broke the 34-year-old record for most home runs in a season set by the great Babe Ruth.

Ruth set the record at 60 homers at the end of the 1927 season. During the next three decades a handful of players would come close, but none were able to reach 60 until 1961, when Maris not only hit 60 homers but then belted his sixty-first home run during the last game of the season. Says *Sporting News* columnist Lisa Olson, "Maris' belting of 61 home runs in a single season [is] a regal record that stood for 37 years before it was washed away in a sea of controversy."[1]

Maris's record lasted longer than Ruth's. But in 1998 two sluggers, Sammy Sosa of the Chicago Cubs and Mark McGwire of the St. Louis Cardinals, found themselves competing in a season-long home run derby. Both players broke Maris's record that year—Sosa hit 66, while McGwire slugged 70. And then, three years later Barry Bonds of the San Francisco Giants broke McGwire's record, slugging 73 homers.

For Major League Baseball (MLB), the slugfests staged by Sosa, McGwire, and Bonds were a boon to the sport, guaranteeing sell-out crowds as the players traveled from stadium to sta-

"[Roger] Maris' belting of 61 home runs in a single season [is] a regal record that stood for 37 years before it was washed away in a sea of controversy."[1]

— *Sporting News* columnist Lisa Olson.

dium in pursuit of the single-season home run record. But behind this grand show of slugging prowess, a dirty little secret started to emerge. Evidence surfaced alleging that Sosa, McGwire, and Bonds had received regular injections of anabolic steroids—chemicals that enhanced their physical strength, enabling them to hit balls harder and farther than they would ordinarily be able to do. Without the help of steroids, many of the homers slugged by the three players would likely have died in midflight, ending as routine fly balls caught by outfielders.

Playing While Juiced

The years in which Sosa, McGwire, and Bonds played their best baseball are known as the steroid era, so-called because of the number of players who have admitted to using steroids or are suspected of playing while "juiced." Says Jose Canseco, a former Major League All-Star who admitted to steroid use, "The challenge is

In the eyes of his sons and many other baseball fans, Roger Maris (pictured at Yankee Stadium in 1962) still holds the record for the most home runs hit in a single season. Three players have actually exceeded Maris's numbers but their achievements are tainted by allegations of drug use.

not to find a player who has used steroids. The challenge is to find a player who hasn't."[2]

When Randy Maris and his brother attended the ceremony at Yankee Stadium to honor their father's accomplishment, they insisted that the true holder of baseball's most sacred record remained their father. "Our family feels strongly that this is Dad's record," says Roger Maris Jr. "He earned it the right way."[3]

The use of anabolic steroids without a prescription is illegal. And yet, even though Major League Baseball implemented its first program of random drug testing on players in 2001, use of steroids and other illegal performance-enhancing drugs have continued. Each year, drug tests have uncovered steroid use by at least some players, but many players have evaded the tests. Indeed, the year in which the first drug tests were administered to players is the same year Bonds broke McGwire's record.

The punishment for using drugs in professional baseball typically includes a suspension—as long as 100 games for the season. During suspensions players are not paid, which means they also suffer financial losses for using drugs.

Moreover, performance-enhancing drugs can cause severe physical and mental problems for users. These drugs have been linked to cancer and other illnesses. One of these illnesses, a condition known as "roid rage," can cause users to explode into angry and irrational tantrums. Says former Major League pitching coach Tom House, "The risk-reward isn't worth it. You may get lucky in the short term, but the medium- and long-term effects are if not life threatening, then close to life threatening."[4]

The use of performance-enhancing drugs is not limited to baseball. The other three major professional sports in America—football, basketball, and hockey—have wrestled with the issue after drug abuse among players had surfaced. Illegal drug use in college athletics is known to occur as well. Moreover, Olympic competitors have tested positive for illegal drugs and have been stripped of their medals. Winners of the Tour de France, the premier bicycle race in the world, have been disqualified from the

"The challenge is not to find a player who has used steroids. The challenge is to find a player who hasn't."[2]

— Former Major League All-Star Jose Canseco.

competitions when urine samples taken after the races indicated use of performance-enhancing drugs.

The Competitive Edge

Randy Maris points out that in the years since Major League Baseball implemented a drug testing policy, no player has been able to break his father's record. "Since they started drug testing, where are the numbers now?"[5] he asks.

A decade after the steroid era Major League Baseball and other professional leagues have been unable to eliminate the use of illegal substances among their players even though they regard the issue of performance-enhancing drugs as serious. Given the rich rewards that can be earned in professional sports—multimillion-dollar contracts from their teams as well as lucrative endorsement deals from commercial interests—many players are willing to take the risk and continue to rely on performance-enhancing drugs to give them an edge over the competition.

Facts

- Barry Bonds weighed 185 pounds (84 kg) in 1986, his rookie season. In 2001, the year he broke the single-season home run record, he weighed 228 pounds (103 kg)—prompting suspicion that he used steroids to help develop muscle, which weighs more than other human tissue.

- Since 2002, as Major League Baseball ramped up its tests for steroids and other drugs, the most home runs any player has hit in a single season is 58—a feat accomplished by Ryan Howard of the Philadelphia Phillies in 2006.

What Is the Origin of the Drug Use Controversy in Sports?

A professional hockey team always has at least one player whose role is that of the "enforcer." The job of these players is to harass the opposing scorers by any means possible—usually by employing their superior size and strength to crash into their opponents, inflicting as much pain as possible. Many of them intentionally start fights, hoping to land punishing punches on the opposing players. For 13 years, Georges Laraque played that role for four teams in the National Hockey League (NHL) before retiring in 2010.

A year after his retirement, Laraque published a biography in which he describes how many NHL enforcers manage to stay at the top of their games: They take steroids to build up their muscles. With more muscle mass, these players are also better able to endure pain when it is dished out by their opponents. "Before a game, as I would warm up on the ice, I would always look at the tough guy on the other side. If his arms were trembling, if his eyes were bulging, I knew for sure he wasn't going to feel any of the punches I would give him," Laraque says. "I knew the guy would be able to take a lot more hits than his fair share."[6]

Laraque says that during his pro hockey career he never used steroids. Moreover, in his book he declines to name the players he knew to be taking performance-enhancing drugs. Nevertheless, Laraque insists that steroid use is common in the NHL. "The job was hard and harsh enough not to have to compete against 'killers' swollen with steroids," Laraque says. "The use of steroids by tough guys makes it unfair for the ones who decide to remain clean."[7]

Element of Danger

Laraque's allegations of widespread steroid use in the NHL should come as no surprise. Performance-enhancing drugs have been a part of the sporting world since the dawn of competitive athletics. Over the years, sports officials have concocted numerous strategies in an effort to keep drugs out of their leagues—the NHL instituted drug testing in 2005—but most plans have fallen short of success. Many players are able to find ways to obtain the drugs and fool the testing authorities. Write Vanderbilt University physicians Andrew J.M. Gregory and Robert W. Fitch, authors of a 2007 study into drug use in sports, "Performance-enhancing drugs . . . have been a part of sports since sporting competition began and likely will be."[8]

Evidence of drug use in athletics dates back to ancient times. The first Olympic games were staged nearly 3,000 years ago in Greece. The competitions included foot races, wrestling matches, long jumps, javelin throws, discus throws, chariot races, and other events. To find extra strength or speed, the ancient Greek athletes were known to consume opium or herbs they believed would enhance their durability. "We've never had clean sport,"[9] insists Charles E. Yesalis, a professor of health and human development at Pennsylvania State University.

In the late nineteenth century, French bicycle racers were known to chew coca leaves—the source of cocaine—to fight off

> "Performance-enhancing drugs . . . have been a part of sports since sporting competition began and likely will be."[8]
>
> — Andrew J.M. Gregory and Robert W. Fitch, authors of a 2007 study into drug use in sports.

fatigue. In the early years of the twentieth century, Olympic athletes used the stimulant strychnine (the key ingredient in rat poison) for an extra boost of energy. In the 1950s, Italian athletes used amphetamines for extra pep while Soviet weight lifters took injections of the male hormone testosterone, believing the hormone added strength to their muscles.

The use of these drugs and others included an element of danger. At the 1960 Olympics in Rome, Danish cyclist Knut Jensen collapsed during his competition, striking his head on the road surface. He suffered a fractured skull and died. An autopsy revealed that he had taken amphetamines before the race, which may have caused him to black out and fall off his bicycle.

Death on the Tour de France

Amphetamines are stimulants. They elevate mood, increase feelings of well-being, and increase energy and alertness. A common—and legal—use of the drug is to treat people who suffer from attention deficit hyperactivity disorder, or ADHD. People afflicted with ADHD are often unable to stay focused, pay attention, and control their behavior. Under law, amphetamines cannot be obtained without a prescription—meaning a physician must monitor the use and effects of the drug on the patient.

Clearly, no physician was monitoring Jensen's use of amphetamines as he participated in the 1960 Olympics. British cyclist Tommy Simpson was also using amphetamines without the guidance of a physician when he competed in the 1967 Tour de France. The world's most famous bicycle race, the Tour de France is a grueling, midsummer event that requires competitors to race some 2,100 miles (3,479 km) over a three-week span. During the 1967 Tour, Simpson and the other racers were required to scale Mont Ventroux, a rocky mountain in the French Alps that lacks shade trees, exposing the competitors to the broiling hot July sun. Making the trek even more challenging was the thick dust that constantly blew across the road. To give himself extra energy to climb Mont Ventroux, Simpson consumed amphetamines before the race that morning.

As the competition got underway, Simpson was in seventh place and among the leaders. He hoped to close the gap on Mont Ventroux but instead found himself falling behind. Two miles from the summit, Simpson started weaving erratically from one side of the road to the other. With a mile to go, Simpson fell off his bicycle. As a crowd gathered around him, Simpson gasped, "Put me back on my bloody bike."[10] Several fans picked him up off the road, helped him back onto his bike, then gave him a push. Simpson wobbled on for a few hundred more feet then fell off his bike again. Now unconscious, Simpson was rushed to a nearby hospital, where he was pronounced dead shortly after arrival. An investigation into the case revealed that the amphetamines Simpson ingested before the race caused him to push his body harder than it was capable of performing.

Baseball and Greenies

The Jensen and Simpson cases occurred in international competitions—far from the purview of American sports fans. Moreover, their deaths occurred during long-distance bicycling competitions—a sport that many Americans do not follow. However, Americans would soon learn about the use of performance-enhancing drugs in their own national pastime—Major League Baseball.

In 1970 Americans were told about drug use in baseball when Major League pitcher Jim Bouton published a bestselling book titled *Ball Four*. The book recounts a season Bouton spent as a member of the Seattle Pilots—an expansion team that later moved to Milwaukee and changed its name to the Brewers. The book was intended as a humorous but honest insider's look at life in the big leagues, but Bouton also reported on the widespread use of amphetamines by players.

In the book, Bouton admits to using amphetamines and names several players who also used the drug to gain a competitive edge. The players swallowed the pills—known around baseball locker rooms as "greenies"—to make themselves more alert, enhance their energy, and improve their levels of concentration. These are important traits for a hitter who must make a split-second decision on whether to swing at a pitch. Pitchers use amphetamines to gain endurance and improve their concentration as well, helping them focus on throwing balls at precise places across the plate where hitters are apt to be fooled. In the book, Bouton makes it crystal clear that the players were using amphetamines illegally and that no doctors were monitoring their use of the drugs. Writes Bouton, "We've been running short of greenies. We don't get them from the trainer, because greenies are against club policy. So we get them from players on other teams who have friends who are doctors, or friends who know where to get greenies. One of our lads is going to have a bunch of greenies mailed to him by some of the guys on the [Boston] Red Sox."[11]

Baseball executives reacted harshly to the book, insisting that the use of amphetamines by players was not as widespread as Bouton contended. Clearly, they were primarily interested in preserving the image of baseball as a wholesome family-friendly sport. Baseball commissioner Bowie Kuhn summoned Bouton to his office for a tongue-lashing. "I advised Mr. Bouton of my displeasure with these writings and have warned him against future writings of this character,"[12] declared Kuhn. But other players soon admitted to using amphetamines as well as other drugs. Darryl Strawberry, a star outfielder for the New York Mets in the 1980s, admitted to taking amphetamines—as well as drugs for recreational purposes, including cocaine and marijuana. "I know that probably nine out of 10 players were taking greenies when I was playing,"[13] said Strawberry.

Football and Bennies

Had Major League Baseball taken Bouton's book seriously and instituted a drug testing policy, the league might have avoided the steroid scandals that came later. But league officials chose to ignore the statements in *Ball Four*, insisting that Bouton had embellished the truth. With no drug testing program in place, in the ensuing years more and more players started relying on performance-enhancing drugs.

Ironically, Bouton was not the only athlete to publish a book in 1970 alleging widespread drug use in sports. Dave Meggyesy, who played linebacker for the National Football League (NFL) Cardinals—then based in St. Louis—published a book titled *Out of Their League* in which he claims that Benzedrine, a form of amphetamine, was used extensively by players. Meggyesy writes that he took his first "bennie" just before playing in a college all-star game. "We got on the bus that was to take us to Kezar Stadium, and as we approached the outskirts of San Francisco I realized the pill was beginning to work. It was as if I were Clark Kent, had slipped into a phone booth and become Superman. I was tense and ready to explode with energy yet I felt total control over myself. I was sure I'd be able to do anything I wanted to on the football field."[14] In fact, Meggyesy played so well during the game that he regretted having already signed his professional contract with the Cardinals. Given the intensity of his hits and tackles during

"Greenies" Are an Old Habit in Baseball

Pitcher Jim Bouton's 1970 book *Ball Four* is given credit for exposing the use of amphetamines in baseball, but prior to Bouton's book the use of "greenies" in Major League locker rooms was hardly a secret. Ralph Kiner, a Hall of Fame outfielder for the Pittsburgh Pirates, returned to his team after serving in World War II. After resuming his career, Kiner said he found athletic trainers dispensing amphetamines to players in his team's locker room. "All the trainers in the ballparks had them," Kiner said.

Moreover, Bouton was not even the first author to write about use of greenies in Major League Baseball. In 1960, pitcher Jim Brosnan, who played for four teams from 1954 to 1963, published a book titled *The Long Season* in which he told of amphetamine use by players who used the drugs to find extra energy for games—particularly after a night of drinking. "It *seemed* to help," Brosnan said of amphetamine use. "If you thought it would help, you tried it. I did. But it didn't always help me."

Quoted in Carlos Frias, "Baseball and Amphetamines," *Palm Beach Post*, April 2, 2006. www.palmbeachpost.com.

the all-star game, Meggyesy says he was sure he could have obtained a more lucrative contract from the pro team.

As with Major League Baseball, NFL officials denied Meggyesy's claims of widespread drug use among players. Shortly after Meggyesy's book was published, Washington Redskins head coach George Allen scoffed, "I know we don't have a drug problem. I'm not worried about it."[15]

The BALCO Scandal

Despite the insistence of Kuhn, Allen, and other sports officials, by the 1980s and 1990s it was growing hard for baseball, football, and the other major sports to deny that athletes were using drugs. In 1985 several members of the US bicycling team at the previous year's Olympics in Los Angeles admitted to "blood doping," in which they received transfusions of blood cells under the belief that a higher red blood cell count would provide more oxygen to their muscles during their competitions. In 1999 these allegations and others led the International Olympic Committee (IOC) and several national sporting federations to set up an independent organization, the World Anti-Doping Agency (WADA). For international competitions such as the Olympics, the WADA determines which drugs should be outlawed and sets standards for tests. Some 600 international sports associations adhere to the WADA's policies. In America the US Olympic Committee established the United States Anti-Doping Agency (USADA) in 2000 to work with WADA and head its antidrug campaigns.

Meanwhile, in professional baseball, the steroid scandals would eventually involve other stars besides Sosa, McGwire, and Bonds. In 2002 Ken Caminiti admitted in a magazine interview that he had used steroids in 1996—the year he won the National League MVP Award as a member of the San Diego Padres. A year later an investigation by a grand jury (a panel of citizens selected to hear evidence presented by prosecutors) revealed that a major supplier of steroids to a number of athletes was the San Francisco–based Bay Area Laboratory Cooperative (BALCO). Victor Conte, the head of BALCO, was charged with distributing illegal drugs. Conte, a former rock musician, pleaded guilty and was sentenced to a brief jail term.

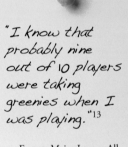

"I know that probably nine out of 10 players were taking greenies when I was playing."[13]

— Former Major League All-Star Darryl Strawberry.

During the grand jury probe, the headlines tended to focus more on the athletes who were alleged to be receiving steroids from BALCO. Eventually, some 30 athletes would be accused of obtaining steroids and similar performance-enhancing drugs through Conte's organization. Among them were Jason Giambi, a former American League MVP; Bill Romanowski, a veteran NFL linebacker who had played in four Super Bowls; Olympic sprinter Marion Jones; and Bonds.

Many of the athletes linked to BALCO were called to testify

before the grand jury. As they gave their testimony, some of the athletes denied using steroids or at least knowing that the substances provided to them by BALCO were banned drugs. Olympic sprinter Kelli White insisted that Conte told her the substances he gave her were vitamins and flaxseed oil. Others who testified were much more defiant. "I have always maintained that I have never ever taken performance-enhancing drugs,"[16] Jones declared to reporters in 2006 as the investigation into BALCO continued. A short time later, Jones was charged with perjury—lying to the grand jury. She pleaded guilty in 2007, tearfully admitting that she had used steroids. Jones was sentenced to six months in prison and stripped of the three gold medals and two bronze medals she won at the 2000 Olympics. On the day of Jones's guilty plea, IOC president Jacques Rogge said, "This is a sad day for sport. The only good that can be drawn from today's revelations is that her decision to finally admit the truth will play, we hope, a key part in breaking the back of the BALCO affair."[17]

The Bonds Conviction

The BALCO investigation continued to turn up evidence of widespread steroid use in sports. Bonds soon found himself under suspicion, and in 2007 he was also charged with lying before the grand jury. Unlike Jones, he continued to maintain his innocence and fought the charges in court. After a three-week trial that began in March 2011, Bonds was convicted by a jury on a single count of obstruction of justice—meaning that rather than lying outright to the grand jury, he nevertheless provided no help to investigators as the grand jury pursued the truth. "He was entirely evasive," says Fred Jacobs, the foreman of the jury that convicted Bonds. "He was often dodging the question. He would just talk about something else."[18] Bonds had also been charged with three counts of perjury, but jurors deadlocked on those charges, unable to come up with unanimous verdicts as required under the law. Prosecutors have indicated they have no plans to retry Bonds on the perjury charges.

In December 2011 Bonds stood for sentencing. Prosecutors asked Judge Susan Illston to sentence Bonds to 15 months in pris-

on. Instead, the judge—noting that Bonds had been convicted of a relatively minor charge—sentenced the now-retired slugger to 30 days of house arrest, meaning he could serve his sentence at home. Soon after Illston handed down the sentence, Bonds's lawyers announced their intentions to appeal his conviction.

San Francisco Giants slugger Barry Bonds smacks a home run in a game against the Oakland A's. Although Bonds was caught up in the BALCO steroid scandal, he has never admitted to using performance-enhancing drugs.

Clemens Called Before Congress

As the BALCO grand jury investigated Bonds and other baseball players, officials of Major League Baseball decided to commission their own investigation of performance-enhancing drug use in their sport. In 2007 league officials retained George Mitchell, a former US senator, to investigate drug use in baseball. Mitchell issued the 400-page report in December 2007, naming 86 Major League players as users of steroids and similar drugs, including seven players who had won Most Valuable Player awards as well as 31 who had played in the sport's All-Star games. Writes Mitchell, "Those who have illegally used these substances range from players whose major league careers were brief to potential members of the Baseball Hall of Fame."[19]

The biggest name in the report was that of pitcher Roger Clemens, winner of seven Cy Young Awards—the highest honor baseball confers annually on pitchers. Clemens's attorney, Rusty Hardin, vehemently denied that his client—by then retired from the game—had used performance-enhancing drugs during his career. "I have great respect for Senator Mitchell," said Hardin.

> I think an overall look at this problem in baseball was an excellent idea but I respectfully suggest it is very unfair to include Roger's name in this report. He is left with no meaningful way to combat what he strongly contends are totally false allegations. He has not been charged with anything, he will not be charged with anything and yet he is being tried in the court of public opinion with no recourse. That is totally wrong.[20]

In 2008 Clemens and his personal trainer Brian McNamee were called before a congressional committee investigating drug use in sports. McNamee testified that on several occasions he injected Clemens with doses of human growth hormone (HGH), a substance that promotes cell growth—an obvious goal among athletes seeking extra muscle mass. Clemens denied the allegations, telling the congressional committee that he had not used performance-enhancing drugs. His denial led to his indictment on several criminal charges of perjury for lying before Congress. He went on trial in 2011, but the case was declared a mistrial after two days because of a mistake in how evidence was presented to the jury by the prosecution. Clemens faced retrial on perjury charges in 2012.

"I know we don't have a drug problem. I'm not worried about it."[15]

— Former Washington Redskins head coach George Allen.

The Stellar Season of Ryan Braun

Throughout the 2000 and 2010 decades, as new and disturbing reports surfaced of drug use by top athletes, sports officials took steps to eliminate the use of performance-enhancing drugs in their leagues. In America all the major professional sports leagues established mandatory drug testing programs as well as penalties—including fines and suspensions—for drug use. Drug testing in collegiate athletics also became mandatory. Despite efforts to stop the use of performance-enhancing drugs by athletes, new cases continue to surface.

In 2011 Milwaukee Brewers outfielder Ryan Braun enjoyed a stellar season, compiling a batting average of .332 while slugging

The First Doping Ban

The first person banned from competitive sports over the use of performance-enhancing drugs is believed to have been James "Choppy" Warburton, who coached British bicycle racers in the late nineteenth century. Warburton was frequently seen at races rushing up to his riders to provide them with drinks from a small black bottle he kept in his pocket. Warburton never disclosed the contents of the bottle, but after ingesting the fluid his riders often found new bursts of energy.

After two incidents in 1897, authorities banned Warburton from bicycle racing in England. In one incident, Warburton's cyclist Arthur Linton seemed to be glassy-eyed and shaky on his bike, yet he won the race in record time. In another case, Warburton's cyclist Jimmy Michael did not lead the race but remained far back in the field. After the race, charges surfaced that Warburton doped Michael to slow him down because Michael was being courted to join a competing team. After his ban from English racing Warburton briefly coached cyclists in France but soon died at the age of 54.

33 homers and 111 runs batted in. He also stole 33 bases. Those statistics helped Braun win the National League MVP Award—an honor that was announced by the league on November 22. Less than three weeks later, baseball officials disclosed that Braun had tested positive for using a synthetic form of the male hormone testosterone and would face a 50-game suspension in 2012. Athletes believe a boost in their testosterone levels will help them gain strength, endurance, and speed.

"I have always maintained that I have never ever taken performance-enhancing drugs."[16]

— Marion Jones, former Olympic sprinter and convicted perjurer.

Braun maintained his innocence, contending that he had never juiced. He appealed his suspension and was granted a hearing before MLB arbitrator Shyam Das. Shortly before players were scheduled to report for spring training in 2012 Das overturned the suspension, permitting Braun to play the entire season for the Brewers. Braun said he felt vindicated by Das's ruling. "It's been an extremely difficult, challenging time in my life," Braun said. "But at the end of the day, I know the truth. My friends, family, teammates, the Milwaukee Brewers organization and everybody who knows me, knows the truth."[21]

An Air of Doubt

Despite Braun's insistence that he never took synthetic testosterone, Das's ruling did not conclude that the player provided a clean urine sample. Instead, Das overturned the suspension because he determined that the lab technician who took the sample failed to follow proper testing procedures. Under MLB rules, the technician is supposed to send the player's urine sample directly to the lab for testing. In the Braun case, the technician believed he had missed the last opportunity to ship the sample before the weekend to the testing lab, which is located in Montreal, Canada. Instead he took the sample home and placed it in his refrigerator where it remained until the following Monday. After 44 hours in the technician's refrigerator, the sample was removed and sent to the lab, which turned up evidence of drug use by Braun.

Das declared the so-called "chain of custody" had been violated, meaning that the sample had not been kept in a secure place from the moment it was collected until it finally arrived at the lab. Theoretically, Das's ruling suggested, someone could have tampered with the sample while it was in the technician's home refrigerator. Therefore, Das ruled, the credibility of the test could be called into question. MLB officials stood by the result of Braun's test. "Major League Baseball runs the highest quality drug testing program of any professional sports organization in the world," [22] declared Rob Manfred, vice president of labor relations for MLB.

As for Braun, as he arrived for spring training he was embraced by his teammates. The 2011 National League MVP may have felt vindicated by the arbitrator's ruling, but given the grounds on which Das ruled—that the sample was left unprotected in a home refrigerator for too long—an air of doubt will always remain over the Braun case.

An Unfair Advantage

Since the dawn of competitive sports, players have always looked for an advantage that would help them run faster, hit their opponents harder, and absorb more punishment to their bodies. In America and elsewhere, top athletes can earn tens of millions of dollars a year while making themselves into celebrities as they enjoy the adoration of their fans. These are clearly incentives that would encourage athletes to rise to the top of their games. Sadly, the evidence has revealed that many players have sought an unfair advantage through the use of performance-enhancing drugs at the risk of public humiliation, imprisonment, and even their own lives.

Facts

- A 2011 poll conducted by the United States Anti-Doping Agency found that 75 percent of sports fans believe the use of performance-enhancing drugs is the most serious problem facing sports.

- A 2011 study of 32 adolescent boys reported in the medical journal *Men and Masculinities* found that most of the study participants believe an athlete with a well-toned and "chiseled" body is likely to be taking performance-enhancing drugs.

- With the conviction of Barry Bonds in 2011, a total of 11 people, including professional athletes, trainers, coaches, and employees of BALCO were convicted on charges stemming from the investigation of the organization.

- To help ensure the 2012 Olympic Games in London, England, were drug-free, housekeepers in the Olympic village were trained to look for discarded needles and other drug paraphernalia as they cleaned the athletes' rooms.

- Five North Korean soccer players tested positive for steroids at the 2011 Women's World Cup. Team officials told the Fédération Internationale de Football Association, the governing body for international soccer, that the players were given the drugs by mistake when they were treated after being struck by lightning earlier in the year.

- According to *Baseball Almanac*, 30 Major League players served suspensions between 2005 and 2011 after testing positive for performance-enhancing drugs.

How Do Performance-Enhancing Drugs Affect Athletes?

Among the many ailments that plague Wayne Coleman is avascular necrosis, which is a deterioration of the bones due to lack of adequate blood supply. The disease causes Coleman to suffer from brittle joints. He has already undergone two hip replacements and has also suffered injuries to his ankles, pelvis, and spine. At the age of 67, he rarely ventures far from his tiny apartment in Phoenix, Arizona, out of fear that he could further damage his fragile body. In 2011 Coleman told a reporter that he does not think he has long to live and has already made his own funeral plans.

Coleman believes his condition is caused by a longtime use of steroids. In the 1970s and 1980s, Coleman was a professional wrestler who performed under the name "Superstar Billy Graham." For decades, pro wrestlers were mostly big, rotund, and rawboned scrappers who performed under such colorful names as George "The Animal" Steele and Andre the Giant. Coleman was first among a new breed of pro wrestlers whose bodies featured sculpted muscles, thin waistlines, and the physiques of ancient gladiators. "I guess I have the dubious title of being the inspirer of many guys to take steroids from that point on in wrestling," says Coleman. "It was just a personal choice for me. The instant gratification and the reward of having that physique made you absolutely blind to the potential side effects or complications."[23]

Although modern professional wrestling is more theater than sport, there is no question that wrestling requires athletic skills. Before finding fame as a wrestler, Coleman spent a brief career in professional football. As a teenager and young adult, he was a dedicated gym rat, spending hours a day lifting weights. It was at a gym in Los Angeles that he met pro wrestler Jerry Graham who invited Coleman to join him on the wrestling circuit as a tag team partner. Coleman adopted the name Billy Graham as part of the act.

While competing on the pro wrestling circuit, he discovered steroids and started injecting himself with the performance-enhancing drugs. He also ingested steroids orally, in pill form. Eventually, he left his tag team partner, established a solo career, added "Superstar" to his ring name, and spent about a year as the champion of the World Wrestling Federation. Meanwhile, over a career that spanned about 10 years, Graham injected himself with steroids hundreds of times while also taking the drugs numerous times by mouth. "I'd always been well-read, and aware of the rumors that steroids could cause long-term health damage," says Coleman. "Yet, after taking massive doses, I'd lie in bed and literally feel my body stretching. It felt so good that I didn't care about the side effects. The mindset was, 'It'll happen to someone else. Not me.'"[24]

Bulging Muscles

Although Coleman may have been exaggerating when he claimed to feel his muscles bulging after a dose of steroids, there is no question that anabolic steroids increase muscle mass and strength. They also have androgenic effects, responsible for enhancing male

Abusing Diuretics: When Athletes Need to Lose Weight

Steroids and similar performance-enhancing drugs help athletes build up muscle mass, which means they gain weight. In some sports—such as amateur wrestling and boxing—athletes must "make weight," meaning they have to remain under a certain weight to compete. To help make weight, many athletes turn to a class of drugs known as diuretics.

These drugs help athletes lose weight by encouraging them to expel fluids from their bodies. In other words, diuretics cause users to urinate. Professional sports leagues in America as well as international sports federations have largely banned diuretics not only because they help athletes make weight through the use of chemicals, but they are often taken as masking agents for steroids and similar drugs. Diuretics help hide the use of steroids by making the athlete expel the banned drugs through urine shortly before a drug test. "Diuretics will cause people to lose fluid, lose weight, and they would effectively be able meet a weight," says John Brewer, head of human performance at the National Sports Centre in Lilleshall, England. "They could help to get rid of the by-products of other, more serious, drugs."

There are some dangers in using diuretics. Abuse of the drugs can lead to dehydration, cramps, dizziness, heat stroke, and low blood pressure.

Quoted in BBC News, "Q&A: Diuretics," February 11, 2003. http://news.bbc.co.uk.

traits—more body hair and deeper voices. The roots of the words anabolic and androgenic can be found in Greek—anabolic means "to build" while androgenic means "masculinizing." The several hundred individual drugs known collectively as steroids are synthetic forms of the male hormone testosterone, which naturally provides these traits in adolescent boys and men. Steroids are known to boost testosterone levels in men to a level 50 times higher than normal.

Steroids can be taken in pill form or injected. Most users inject steroids because when the drug is taken orally it is known to contribute to liver failure. Other side effects of steroid use include brittle bones, acne, rapid weight gain, reduced sperm count, erectile dysfunction, shrinking of testicles, and painful urination, among other ills. "There can be a whole panoply of side effects, even with prescribed doses," says Gary Wadler, a professor at New York University School of Medicine. "Some are visible to the naked eye and some are internal. Some are physical, others are psychological. With unsupervised steroid use, wanton 'megadosing' or stacking—using a combination of different steroids—the effects can be irreversible or undetected until it's too late."[25]

One of the most popular steroids among athletes is androstenedione, commonly known as "andro," which is the steroid that Mark McGwire used during his career. Side effects of andro include acne, diminished sperm production, shrinkage of the testicles, and enlargement of the breasts. It also causes hair to fall out. Andro also decreases levels of good cholesterol, which can lead to heart attack and stroke.

There are many legitimate uses for the drugs when they are obtained with prescriptions and administered under the supervision of physicians. Steroids contain anti-inflammatory properties and have been used to treat asthma, an inflammation of the airways in the lungs, as well as arthritis, a painful inflammation of the joints. The muscle-building qualities of steroids have helped muscular dystrophy patients, who suffer from a disease that causes deterioration of their muscles. Men who have suffered from testicular cancer often lack the hormone testosterone. Steroids have been prescribed to boost testosterone levels in these patients.

"With unsupervised steroid use, wanton 'megadosing' or stacking—using a combination of different steroids—the effects can be irreversible or undetected until it's too late."[25]

— New York University School of Medicine professor Gary Wadler.

Women and Steroids

If steroids provide bulging muscles, more body hair, deeper voices and other masculine traits in the men who consume the drug, what happens to women who take steroids? Andreas Krieger can answer that question. The moustache-wearing Krieger is a strapping 6 feet 1 inch (1.87 m) in height. He is married and owns a military surplus store in Magdeburg, Germany.

He has built a new life following a sex change operation in 1997. Prior to the procedure Krieger's first name was Heidi, and she was well known in her country as a top Olympic competitor. Indeed, during the 1980s Heidi Krieger was one of the top female shot put athletes in the world, winning a gold medal in the 1986 European championships. She had been trained to compete since childhood and, unknown to her at the time, fed a steady diet of steroids by her coaches. She received daily doses of a steroid in the form of blue pills, which her coaches told her were vitamins.

By the age of 18, Krieger weighed 220 (100 kg) pounds, had

During the Cold War, sports officials in East Germany and other parts of Soviet-controlled Europe routinely gave steroids to women athletes. Steroid use remains a problem in many sports. This Russian shot putter (pictured in 2004) had to forfeit her gold medal after testing positive for banned steroids.

a deep voice and abundant hair on her body—including her face. One day, as she rode a train while wearing a dress, she was ridiculed by other passengers who accused her of being a transvestite—a man who wears women's clothes. "I was no longer Heidi Krieger," says Krieger. "I didn't know anymore who I was . . . I wasn't able to identify with my body anymore."[26] After that train ride, she never wore a dress again.

At the time, Krieger resided in the former East Germany. It was during the era of the Cold War—the time in which the former Soviet Union and its allies attempted to make socialism the dominant culture on earth. Officials of the Soviet satellite country of East Germany formed a plan to make their athletes into top competitors at the Olympics and other international events. They recruited children as young as 11 who had shown athletic promise and enrolled them in special schools in which sports was the predominant component of the curriculum. They aimed to prove that under socialism—state control over virtually all facets of society—young people could excel and grow into world leaders. Part of their plan included feeding steroids to the young athletes.

"It's terrifying what they did to us," said Carola Beraktschjan, a swimmer who, at the age of 14 set a world record in the women's 100-meter breaststroke. "I took up to 30 pills a day. They always told us they were vitamins. There was no question you would not take them. You had to play by the rules. We were vehicles chosen to prove that socialism was better than capitalism. What happened to our bodies was entirely secondary to that political mission."[27]

Infertility, Miscarriages, and Birth Defects

Beraktschjan was a member of the East German swim team that competed at the 1976 Summer Olympics in Montreal, Canada. That year, East German women won 11 of the 13 individual gold medals and set eight world records. US swimmer Wendy Boglioli recalls competing against the East Germans: "They were very strong women; they were very fast; we thought they were machines. Here we were. . . . America's best athletes ever put together on a team, and every single day the East German women were winning every, every event."[28] Overall, East German athletes won 40 gold medals at the 1976 Summer Olympics—an unprecedented achievement for a country of just 17 million people.

In the years following their achievements at the Olympics, the East German women noticed strange changes to their bodies: They grew excessive body hair and developed deep voices. Fifteen of the athletes suffered from either infertility or miscarriages. Those who did give birth found that some of their babies suffered from birth defects. As six of the athletes grew into adolescence, they failed to develop breasts. Indeed, as many as 2,000 former East German athletes are believed to be suffering from cancer, heart disease, infertility, and depression as a result of their steroid-laden diets. Says swimmer Katharina Bullin, "Injections, pills, it was all normal. . . . Nothing strange about it and I wouldn't have known what to ask because I wasn't skeptical at all. I didn't start to look like a man overnight, it happened gradually. I wasn't really aware of it myself but it was obvious to everyone else. And whether I wore a dress or a skirt, makeup or jewelry, it got worse and worse. They called me a transvestite or gay, and it shocked me."[29]

The Soviet Union collapsed in 1991 and with it, the dreams of its leaders to spread socialism to the West. The countries that had been under Soviet domination broke away to form new governments. Germany, which had been divided into two countries at the end of World War II, reunited into a single nation. Soon, the secrets of how the East German athletes won all those gold medals began to surface. And the women who were affected brought charges against the former East German sports officials who had been secretly feeding them heavy doses of steroids.

In 2000 two former East German sports officials were convicted of endangering the lives of the athletes who spent their childhood years consuming diets of performance-enhancing drugs. Neither Manfred Ewald, national minister of sports, nor Manfred Hoeppner, a physician who oversaw the steroids program, was made to serve jail time—an outcome of the case that many former East German athletes found disturbing. As for Krieger, he says he finds it even more disturbing that today's athletes, includ-

"I was no longer Heidi Krieger. I didn't know anymore who I was . . . I wasn't able to identify with my body anymore."[26]

— Former East German Olympic athlete Andreas Krieger, who underwent a sex change operation after years of taking steroids.

ing women, take steroids with full knowledge of the terrible side effects of the drugs. "If today's athletes say they want to take the risk, they really don't know what risk they are taking,"[30] he says.

Human Growth Hormone

In the years since athletes like Coleman and Krieger ingested steroids, other performance-enhancing drugs have been discovered by athletes, many of whom have been anxious to consume them in search of a competitive edge over their opponents. Similar to anabolic steroids, human growth hormone (HGH), also known as gonadotropin, improves muscle mass and endurance. Athletes

Is 'Roid Rage Real?

Physicians warn that a dangerous side effect of steroid use is aggressive behavior—that athletes and others who abuse steroids can lose their tempers, lash out at others, and are capable of violence. The condition is known as 'roid rage. "People's psychological states can run the gamut," says New York University School of Medicine professor Gary Wadler. "They can go from bouts of depression or extreme irritability to feelings of invincibility and outright aggression, commonly called 'roid rage. This is a dangerous state beyond mere assertiveness."

One person who disagrees is Hulk Hogan, the former pro wrestling champion. Hogan, who has admitted to taking steroids during his wrestling career, says he knew many wrestlers who took the drugs and never encountered anyone in a steroid-induced rage. "The fact is, I've been around more steroid users than the average person in my lifetime, and 'roid rage is something I have never, ever seen," says Hogan. "It's certainly nothing I've ever felt. I almost think it's some sort of an urban myth."

Quoted in ESPN, "Anabolic Steroids," September 6, 2007. http://espn.go.com.
Hulk Hogan and Mark Dagostino, "As Real as Real Gets," *Men's Fitness*, November 2009, p. 78.

who have admitted to using HGH include former New York Yankees pitcher Andy Pettitte, who retired after the 2010 season, and infielder Chuck Knoblauch, who enjoyed a 12-year Major League career with three teams before retiring after the 2002 season. According to the Mitchell report, Roger Clemens also used HGH and in the federal charges brought against Barry Bonds, prosecutors alleged the slugger used HGH to enhance his performance.

HGH users may experience two conditions that could lead to heart failure: hyperlipidemia, which increases the fat content of the blood, and cardiomyopathy, a disease of the heart in which the organ grows larger and more rigid. In addition, abusers may see their hands, feet, and heads grow larger. A condition known as "lantern jaw," in which the lower jaw protrudes beyond the upper jaw, is common among HGH abusers. Says Joseph Fetto, an assistant professor of sports medicine at New York University, "It's known in medicine that a small number of individuals secrete too much growth hormone, which in adulthood can lead to a bizarre growth of the jaw, feet and bones. . . . There are no beneficial effects from its use with athletes except putting on weight."[31]

As with steroids, HGH has a legitimate use: It is employed to treat a condition known as bone dysplasia in children. Young children who suffer from the disease may not grow into full-size adults and instead face a life of dwarfism.

More Oxygen for Muscles

Athletes use HGH and steroids to help them achieve common goals: to boost the size of their muscles, add weight, and provide them with more strength and endurance. Other drugs also help athletes gain strength and endurance by providing more oxygen to the blood, which in turn supplies more oxygen to the muscles—making them stronger. One drug used by athletes to increase the oxygen supply to their blood and therefore their muscles is erythropoietin, also known as EPO.

EPO is a popular drug in the international cycling community. Among the cyclists who have tested positive for the drug are Spaniard Mikel Astarloza and Italians Pasquale Muto and Ricardo Ricco. In fact, Ricco was competing in the 2008 Tour de France when he tested positive for the drug. He had won two of the 20 stages of the race and was in ninth place just prior to the start of the twelfth stage when he was disqualified.

EPO is a legitimate drug therapy for patients whose kidneys develop anemia—a lack of blood which can lead to kidney failure. The danger to athletes who abuse EPO is that the drug will cause them to push their bodies too hard, causing stroke or heart failure. EPO first surfaced as a dangerous performance-enhancing drug in the early 1990s when several top international cyclists suffered heart failures, including 27-year-old Dutch cyclist Johannes Draaijer, who died of a heart attack in his sleep just a few days after a competition. Said the late Edmund Burke, who coached the US Olympic cycling team in 1980 and 1984, "EPO can do wonders for your aerobic capacity. The problem is, it can also kill you."[32]

Blood Doping

Some athletes have found ways to provide more oxygen to their muscles without the use of performance-enhancing drugs by undergoing the process known as "blood doping." In blood doping, red blood cells are added to the athlete's blood, providing more oxygen to the muscles. Typically, a month or more before a competition, an athlete will have up to four units of blood (about 60 ounces or 1,800 ml) withdrawn from his or her body. A technician will use a centrifuge to separate the red blood cells from the sample, then place the cells in cold storage until shortly before the competition. As the day of the race nears, the blood cells are injected into the athlete's body. Some athletes do not use their own blood cells but are injected with cells from donors who have similar blood types.

Blood doping is popular among athletes who compete in endurance events, such as bicycle racing and cross-country skiing competitions. In 2011 American cyclist Tyler Hamilton admitted during a TV interview that he added red cells to his blood during the 2004 Olympics. Following the interview, Hamilton returned the gold medal he won in the competition.

Blood doping can be dangerous—the process tends to make the blood "sludgy," meaning it does not travel freely through the veins. That makes the heart work harder, which can cause heart failure and death. In 2008, 19-year-old Russian hockey player Alexei Cherepanov—a top prospect for the New York Rangers of the National Hockey League—died shortly after collapsing during a game in Moscow. An investigation into the young star's death

Alexei Cherepanov smiles broadly after being selected to play for the New York Rangers ice hockey team in 2007. Cherepanov, 19, died the following year after he collapsed during a game in Moscow. An investigation revealed that he had been blood doping for months.

revealed he had been blood doping for months and, in fact, had received a transfusion on the day of his death.

The Strong Grip of Performance-Enhancing Drugs

Former athletes like Coleman, Krieger, and Bullin provide living examples of what can go wrong when athletes use performance-enhancing drugs. In many ways these athletes can regard themselves as fortunate because they have survived as long as they have. In contrast, Cherepanov died at the age of 19 long before he fulfilled his enormous potential in professional hockey or even had an opportunity to play the game at its highest level. Draaijer also had a top career in international bicycle racing cut short, losing his life in the prime of his competitive years.

Many other athletes have also lost their lives after years of abusing performance-enhancing drugs. One case that stands out is that of Lyle Alzado, a former NFL lineman who died of cancer at the age of 43 after years of injecting himself with steroids and HGH. He also ingested steroids orally. While playing for the Raiders, then located in Los Angeles, Alzado continued taking performance-enhancing drugs even though the team's doctor, Robert Huizenga, discovered Alzado's drug use through a routine blood test. Huizenga said he advised Alzado in the strongest possible words that his use of steroids and HGH was potentially life-threatening and he should stop immediately. Alzado's career spanned from 1971 to 1985; at the time, the NFL had no mandatory drug-testing policy nor did it penalize players for taking performance-enhancing drugs. According to Huizenga, Alzado refused to stop using steroids and HGH, arguing that he needed them to maintain his competitive edge. Alzado later said he spent as much as $30,000 a year during his career buying steroids and HGH.

Even after retiring from the game, Alzado continued working out, lifting weights and taking steroids. As someone who had been a top athlete for all his adult life, Alzado could not bear the thought of losing his athletic physique. And then, in 1991, he

"[Erythropoietin] can do wonders for your aerobic capacity. The problem is, it can also kill you."[32]

— Former US Olympic cycling coach Edmund Burke.

fainted on the street. After a series of tests, he was diagnosed with brain cancer. "I know there's no written, documented proof that steroids and human growth hormone caused this cancer," Alzado said after he was diagnosed with brain cancer, "but it's one of the reasons you have to look at. You have to."[33]

Alzado died less than a year after he wrote those words in a story for *Sports Illustrated*. The year was 1992—more than two decades ago. The fact that his death did not serve to discourage numerous other athletes from experimenting with steroids and similar substances illustrates the strong grip performance-enhancing drugs have on the athletes who take them.

Facts

- The University of Zurich in Switzerland reported in 2011 that long- and short-term use of the performance-enhancing drug erythropoietin may constrict blood vessels in the brain, raising blood pressure and increasing the risk of stroke in users.

- A 2011 study by the Swedish university Karolinska Institute reported that human growth hormone and erythropoietin can combine to form cancerous tumors.

- A 2011 study by Harvard Medical School in Massachusetts evaluated 231 male weightlifters and found that 27 of the athletes, or 12 percent of the study group, had been using both anabolic steroids and human growth hormone.

- The medical journal *Annals of Internal Medicine* reported in 2010 that 96 Australian sprinters injected with human growth hormone over an eight-week period improved their athletic ability, shaving an average of 0.4 seconds off their times in the 100-meter dash.

- Athletes who use performance-enhancing drugs are more likely to also abuse alcohol as well as recreational drugs such as marijuana and cocaine, according to a 2009 study by Rutgers University in New Jersey.

- Steroids taken orally can lead to a vitamin D deficiency, according to a 2011 study by Albert Einstein College of Medicine in New York. A lack of vitamin D can lead to soft bones. Eleven percent of steroid users had vitamin D deficiencies researchers regarded as "severe."

Are Drug Users Cheaters?

Beta blockers fall under a classification of drugs doctors prescribe for patients who suffer from hypertension, also known as high blood pressure. Hypertension can be a deadly condition because it makes the heart work harder, which can result in heart failure. It is a known fact that many of the world's finest classical musicians consume beta blockers before performing, regardless of whether they suffer from hypertension. "These drugs lower heart rate and blood pressure, reducing the physical effects of stress, and it has been shown that the quality of a musical performance is improved if the musician takes these drugs,"[34] state Julian Savulescu, Bennett Foddy, and M. Clayton, bioethics experts and authors of a report on drug use in sports.

Therefore, the authors argue, if it is acceptable for the world's best musicians to take drugs to improve their performances, why is it unacceptable for the world's top athletes to improve their performances with the help of drugs? "Although elite classical music is arguably as competitive as elite sport, and the rewards are similar, there is no stigma attached to the use of these drugs," report the three authors. "We do not think less of the violinist or pianist who uses them."[35]

Savulescu, Foddy, Clayton, and other experts argue that instead of providing athletes with unfair advantages over their competitors, drugs should be regarded as a method to level the playing

> "If it's wrong for athletes to use performance-enhancing drugs, there must be something wrong about sport that makes it so."[37]
>
> — Bioethics expert Thomas H. Murray.

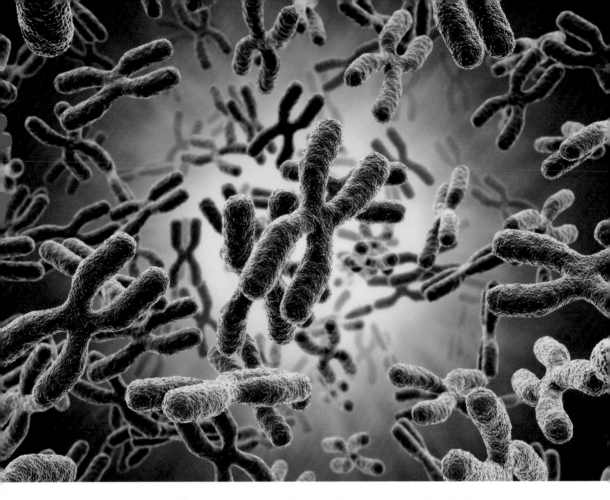

Genetics (represented by this computer illustration of chromosomes) play a huge role in athletic prowess. Some experts contend that performance-enhancing drugs actually level the playing field rather than giving one athlete an unfair advantage over another.

field. They contend that to play at the top level of any sport, an athlete must train hard, enlist the aid of good coaches, and have access to the best equipment. But there is also another component to athletic prowess, and that component is genetic: Thanks to their ancestors, all top athletes are born with the DNA that guarantees they will mature into bigger, stronger, and faster specimens than ordinary people. "People do well at sport as a result of the genetic lottery that happened to deal them a winning hand," the report's authors write. "Sport discriminates against the genetically unfit. Sport is the province of the genetic elite."[36]

Regulate, Not Ban, Drug Use

Savulescu, Foddy, and Clayton are not alone in their call to legalize performance-enhancing drugs. As athletes continue to be caught using steroids and similar drugs, a growing body of advocates argues that the sports leagues would benefit by closing down their various efforts to eliminate drugs and instead find ways to regulate their use and ensure they are administered under the authority of physicians. Thomas H. Murray, president of the Hastings Center, a Garrison, New York–based bioethics center, says the sporting world has often welcomed innovation. He cites such examples as the development of larger baseball gloves, replacement of bamboo poles with fiberglass poles in the sport of pole vaulting, and even innovations in the materials used to manufacture swimsuits that have helped improve the performance of swimmers. He says performance-enhancing drugs should be regarded as another innovation. "The mere fact that some drugs enhance performance isn't sufficient to decide whether they are good, bad or otherwise," insists Murray. "If it's wrong for athletes to use performance-enhancing drugs, there must be something wrong about sport that makes it so."[37]

And journalist Matthew Herper, who covers medical issues for *Forbes* magazine, says,

> To me, the most obvious solution has always been to legalize those drugs that work, and to experimentally monitor new entrants . . . for both efficacy and safety. Biological improvement would be treated much as athletic equipment like baseball bats and running shoes. This could improve both [the] athlete's performance and their health, and would be a lot better than having everybody trying whatever additive they can sneak [and] attempting to stay ahead of drug tests.[38]

If the sports world were to adopt the policies recommended by Murray, Herper, and the other experts, it would require a fundamental shift in the universal attitude among league officials, fans, and even the athletes themselves: The use of performance-enhancing drugs is cheating. That viewpoint is regularly and emphatically voiced by league officials. "The integrity of the NFL is critical," NFL commissioner Roger Goodell told an interviewer in 2011. "We have

"At first I felt like a cheater. If a young player were to ask me what to do, I'm not going to tell him it's bad."[43]

— Ken Caminiti, who used steroids the year he won the National League MVP award.

to make sure that we're doing everything possible to have the best drug program in sports. We would be naïve to think that people aren't going to cheat the system, but we have to have the best drug testing program to be able to offset it."[39]

Fans also appear unwilling to accept the notion that performance-enhancing drugs could be made an acceptable part of sports. A 2009 poll by Marist University in New York reported that nearly 60 percent of respondents question the credibility of baseball records because of steroid use by players. Moreover, 53 percent of respondents said they believe there have been more home runs hit in recent years because the players are juicing.

Players know the credibility of sports has been hurt because the public believes many athletes are cheating. "We definitely care what the fans think because we don't do what we do without the fans,"[40] says Josh Beckett, a pitcher for the Boston Red Sox. Political leaders have also weighed in. US senator John McCain of Arizona has threatened to write legislation mandating that all sports leagues impose drug-testing programs if they fail to establish testing programs on their own. "What do we do?" McCain asks. "It seems to me that we ought to seriously consider . . . a law that says all professional sports have a minimum level of performance-enhancing drug testing."[41]

When Drug Use Was Permitted

The use of drugs in sports was not always regarded as cheating. In 1904 American track star Thomas Hicks consumed a glass of brandy laced with the stimulant strychnine before competing in that year's Olympic marathon. Four miles from the end of the grueling race, Hicks signaled to his trainer that he was running out of energy. The trainer rushed to Hicks with another glass of brandy laced with strychnine. Hicks consumed the concoction, then pushed on, crossing the finish line in second place. (Minutes later, he collapsed from exhaustion and never competed again.) Later, Hicks was awarded the gold medal because the winner, American Fred Lorz, was found to have traveled in a car for 11 of the marathon's 26 miles. And so, at the time, Lorz was branded a cheater because he rode in a car for nearly half the race, but Hicks

Tiger Woods and LASIK Surgery

Golfer Tiger Woods was on a streak of bad luck in 1999, losing 16 straight tournaments. To improve his game, Woods underwent surgery to correct his vision. After the surgery, he won seven of his next 10 tournaments. Today, Woods is ranked among the top golfers in the world.

Prior to the surgery Woods was severely nearsighted—able to clearly see objects that were no more than a foot away. He had difficulty seeing distant objects—a handicap for golfers who strive to hit specific places on the fairway that are often hundreds of yards away. Woods found eyeglasses and contact lenses little help, so he underwent surgery known as laser-assisted in situ keratomileusis, or LASIK, a procedure in which a physician uses a laser to reshape the corneas. After the surgery, Woods's vision improved to 20/15, meaning he could see at a distance of 20 feet what most other people see at 15 feet.

Critics wonder why a performance-enhancing procedure such as LASIK is permitted in sports but using drugs to help enhance an athlete's performance is considered cheating. "Mark McGwire was hauled before a congressional hearing and lambasted as a cheater [for using steroids]," says *Slate* columnist William Saletan. "Tiger Woods was celebrated for winning golf's biggest tournament, the Masters, with the help of superior vision he acquired through laser surgery. What's the difference?"

William Saletan, "The Beam in Your Eye: If Steroids Are Cheating, Why Isn't LASIK?," *Slate*, April 18, 2005. www.slate.com.

was declared a champion, even though he ran the race under the influence of a chemical stimulant.

Outlawing the use of drugs in sports is, actually, a relatively new development. The first drug tests were administered to athletes in 1968 at the Winter Olympics in Grenoble, France. Officials took urine samples at random from some of the competitors, seeking evidence of the use of stimulants, such as amphetamines. It was highly suspected that many athletes were using steroids, but at the time a test had not yet been developed that could detect the substances. Nevertheless, officials tested 86 athletes and found no evidence of drugs in the samples. Later that year, at the Summer Olympics in Mexico City, officials tested 667 athletes and turned up one positive test.

Over the years, as medical science has improved, better drug testing techniques have developed. And as drug testing techniques have improved—and, therefore, uncovered more cases—society has taken a dim view of the athletes who use performance-enhancing drugs. Meanwhile, the various professional, college, and international leagues have set their own policies. The International Olympic Committee (IOC) will strip athletes of their medals if they are found to be using drugs. But in Major League Baseball, the records of Barry Bonds, Sammy Sosa, Roger Clemens, and Mark McGwire are permitted to stand even though the evidence has strongly pointed to their use of performance-enhancing drugs during their careers.

Punishing the Users

To punish drug users, most leagues have adopted a series of fines and suspensions, depending on the circumstances. Baseball's current rules call for a 50-game suspension for the first offense, 100-game suspension for the second offense, and lifetime suspension for the third offense. During their suspensions, the players do not receive their salaries—an economic penalty that could mean millions of dollars to star players. These penalties could be considered harsh, but a player who sits out a 50- or 100-game suspension returns to the lineup following his suspension with the same batting average or earned run average he compiled before his drug test came back positive.

Therefore, even though the player cheated, his steroid-assisted accomplishments on the field are permitted to stand. In baseball, critics consider it to be a hypocritical policy and have called for baseball commissioner Bud Selig to wipe out Bonds's records as well as the records compiled by others who have taken steroids. Says *USA Today* sports columnist Christine Brennan, "We know what Major League Baseball commissioner Bud Selig is going to do about Barry Bonds' embarrassing home run records. He will do nothing. He will let Bonds' single-season home run record of 73 and career record of 762 sit there and fester until they are broken—which could very well be never now that baseball is doing some pretty serious drug testing."[42] In a 2011 interview with journalists shortly after Bonds was convicted of obstruction of justice, Selig brushed off questions about whether he would consider erasing the slugger's records, refusing to give a reason why he has decided to let Bonds's achievements remain on the books.

In contrast, the IOC will strip competitors of their medals if their drug tests come back positive. Moreover, the gold medal stripped from a drug user will be awarded to the second-place finisher. Therefore, the IOC wipes the slate clean—erasing the records of the drugged athlete.

Accusing Lance Armstrong of Doping

Athletes who have come clean about their drug use have admitted they felt like cheaters when they juiced up. "At first I felt like a cheater," said Ken Caminiti, who used steroids the year he won the National League MVP award. "If a young player were to ask me what to do, I'm not going to tell him it's bad. Look at all the money in the game: You have the chance to set your family up, to get your daughter into a better school. . . . So I can't say, 'Don't do it,' when the guy next to you is as big as a house and he's going to take your job and make the money."[43] Caminiti died in 2004 at the age of 41 from a heart attack after years of fighting a cocaine addiction.

Even an unproven accusation that a sports star has used performance-enhancing drugs has forced many athletes into struggles to escape the label of cheater. In 2006 American cyclist Floyd Landis won the Tour de France but shortly after the race was stripped of the title when a test indicated he had been blood doping. Landis spent the next four years denying the allegation. He even published a book in 2007, titled *Positively False*, in which he

made a strong case that testing procedures are faulty. But finally, in 2010 Landis owned up to the charge and admitted to blood doping and using performance-enhancing drugs.

But Landis did much more than admit to his own drug use—he charged that other American cyclists were also guilty of using performance-enhancing drugs. Among the cyclists accused by Landis was Lance Armstrong, an icon of American sports. Armstrong started his career in bicycle racing in 1991 and by 1993 was one of the top riders on the international circuit. In 1996 he was diagnosed with testicular cancer. Armstrong was given little chance to survive the disease, but after surgery and intensive chemotherapy treatments he recovered and, remarkably, returned to competitive cycling. Moreover, Armstrong won the Tour de France in 1999 and then went on to win another six consecutive Tours. In 1999, after his first Tour win, he was feted at the White House. "You captured the eyes of the nation and the hearts of the entire world,"[44] said vice president Al Gore. In 2002, after his fourth win in the Tour de France, *Sports Illustrated* named Armstrong to its coveted recognition as "Sportsman of the Year."

Living Under Suspicion

In the months following Landis's charges against Armstrong, other cycling veterans stepped forward and supported the accusations. "I saw EPO in [Armstrong's] refrigerator," Tyler Hamilton told interviewers for the CBS News show *60 Minutes* in 2011. "I saw him inject it more than one time—like we all did. Like I did, many, many times."[45] The accusations by Landis, Hamilton, and others led prosecutors to impanel a grand jury to investigate Armstrong on charges of fraud, trafficking in illegal drugs, and other charges. Armstrong's cycling team was sponsored by the US Postal Service, which invested $40 million in the team. Investigators want to know if some of that money, which was provided by postal customers, was spent by Armstrong on illegal drugs.

The grand jury started meeting in 2011. As the investigation proceeded, Armstrong maintained his innocence, labeling Landis and the others liars. Armstrong suggested that Landis leveled the charges in order to claim a million-dollar fee from a publisher who offered the money to the disgraced cyclist to write a tell-all book about drug use in cycling. "If you said, 'Give me one word to sum this all up [it is] credibility,'" Armstrong angrily charged. "Floyd lost his credibility a long time ago."[46]

For more than a year, Armstrong lived under the suspicion that he spent a career cheating his way to the top of the international cycling world. "If Armstrong turns out to be a cheat—and it's getting harder to believe him—then he'll have been the worst of them all," says *Sporting News* columnist Greg Couch. "Others juiced to

"Much of [the] risk comes from your ignorance and the dubious grade of steroid you're getting. A star player with access to the best stuff and the best medical supervision isn't taking the same degree of risk."[51]

— *Slate* columnist William Saletan.

win, but if he did it, it was part of his miracle, good-guy image he asked us to believe."[47] And Bill Strickland, the author of a biography of Armstrong, says, "Accepting that Lance cheated makes me want to cry. A 46-year-old guy. Can you imagine that?"[48]

Do Steroid Users Deserve Hall of Fame Consideration?

In 2012 the names of Mark McGwire and Rafael Palmeiro appeared on the ballot for the National Baseball Hall of Fame in Cooperstown, New York. For McGwire, it was his fourth year of eligibility, while for Palmeiro the 2012 election marked his first year on the ballot.

To be eligible for election to the Hall, a player must be retired for at least five years. To win election, a player must garner 75 percent of the 600-some votes cast by American sportswriters. In 2012 McGwire, the one-time holder of the single-season home run mark, received less than 20 percent of the vote. Palmeiro, who slugged 569 career home runs, received less than 13 percent. McGwire has admitted to using steroids, while Palmeiro failed a drug test and was forced to sit out a suspension in 2005, although he has never admitted to steroid use and insists the test results were faulty.

Meanwhile 2013 marks the first year of eligibility for induction for Barry Bonds, Roger Clemens, and Sammy Sosa. *Sporting News* writer Garry Howard echoed the sentiments of many American sportswriters when he said, "I really thought Palmeiro, Bonds and Clemens were first-ballot Hall of Famers until they did the steroid dance. McGwire deserves serious consideration, but his monster year is truly tainted. I did not vote for McGwire or Palmeiro [in 2012] and will not vote for Bonds, Clemens or Sosa."

Quoted in *Sporting News*, "Hall of Fame 2012," January 2012. http://aol.sportingnews.com.

Armstrong was eventually exonerated. In 2012, federal prosecutors announced they had closed the investigation against Armstrong and would not bring charges. Prosecutors refused to comment on why they had closed the probe, but the press reported that throughout his career, Armstrong had never failed a drug test.

Despite the decision by American authorities to drop the investigation of Armstrong, international cycling is still a sport that remains under the cloud of performance-enhancing drug use. In 2012, the Court of Arbitration for Sport in Switzerland—a panel that settles disputes in international competitions and conducts hearings into accusations against athletes—suspended 2010 Tour de France winner Alberto Contador for two years after determining he used the banned muscle-building drug clenbuterol. The court stripped the Spanish cyclist of his Tour victory as well as victories in 17 other races he won since then. "This is a sad day for our sport," says Pat McQuaid, president of the International Cycling Union, the sport's governing body. "There are no winners when it comes to the issue of doping: every case, irrespective of its characteristics, is always a case too many."[49]

Healing with Stem Cells

Athletes like Landis, Hamilton, Contador, and Armstrong have been accused of cheating by taking performance-enhancing drugs or blood doping, but what if an athlete gains a competitive advantage over others through experimental medical procedures that are not widely recognized as acceptable by the mainstream medical or sports communities? Can making use of these therapies be regarded as cheating?

Pitcher Bartolo Colon's best years were behind him when he suddenly reemerged in 2011 with a $900,000 contract to play for the Yankees. At the time, he was 38 years old and had not pitched effectively in six years. In fact, Colon missed the entire 2010 season with an elbow injury. But Colon returned to the big leagues in 2011 with an elbow healed through stem cell therapy. Stem cells are "undifferentiated" cells, meaning they have yet to form into cells that compose blood, tissue, or bone. In this highly experimental therapy, stem cells are injected into the body where they

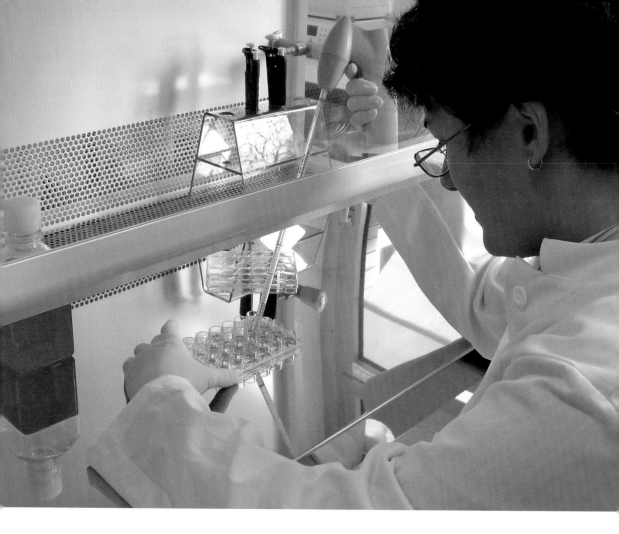

have the potential to grow into mature cells, replacing the damaged cells—in Colon's case, helping to heal his injured elbow. In America, stem cell therapy is very much in the experimental phase and has not been approved by the US Food and Drug Administration as a treatment doctors can prescribe for their patients. Virtually the only patients now receiving stem cell therapy in America are those who participate in clinical trials.

But that is not true in other countries, including the Dominican Republic—which is where Colon received his stem cell therapy. ESPN.com columnist Howard Bryant questions whether Colon has played fair by reviving his career with an experimental therapy that has not been approved for patients—athletes or otherwise—in America. "The real question is where on the continuum of available therapies rehabilitation and recovery ends and gaming the system begins," says Bryant. "One end of the spectrum is Gatorade and aspirin, which are legal, available to everyone and widely used. But it gets murkier as the treatments grow more aggressive, experimental and scarce."[50]

The Spirit of Sport

If Colon has been able to extend his career as a big league pitcher through stem cell therapy, then chances are other professional athletes will soon be seeking similar treatments in the hope that they can also add a few extra seasons to their careers. Given the advancements in science—not only in stem cell therapy but in drug therapy as well—the call to recognize these treatments as legitimate procedures has gained traction in recent years. William Saletan, a columnist for *Slate*, points out that steroids have long been recognized to have legitimate medical uses and are in the vast majority of cases prescribed to patients under the supervision of physicians. As with most pharmaceuticals, he says, steroids and similar drugs are constantly being refined and improved. "Don't get me wrong. If you buy a steroid off the street or the Internet today just to bulk up, you're taking a stupid risk," he says. "But much of that risk comes from your ignorance and the dubious grade of steroid you're getting. A star player with access to the best stuff and the best medical supervision isn't taking the same degree of risk. Furthermore, steroids are a crude, early phase of enhancement technology. Chemists are trying every day to refine compounds and doses that might help pro athletes without bad side effects."[51]

Other experts disagree. Urban Wiesing, a professor of medical ethics at the University of Tuebingen in Berlin, Germany, argues that legalizing performance-enhancing drugs would not level the playing field but rather create a world where fans suspect that superior accomplishments by athletes—record-setting times, electrifying runs for touchdowns, stunning blows by boxers—are accomplished with the help of performance-enhancing drugs. "Crucially, a legalization of performance-enhancing drugs

> "The sports watching audience is interested in athletic performance, not biochemistry."[52]
>
> — Urban Wiesing, professor of medical ethics at the University of Tuebingen in Germany.

would have a massive impact on our perception of sport," he argues. "It would ultimately compromise the currently, widely accepted 'spirit of sport.' Sport is an artificial setting, created by human beings, in which the competitor is required to perform, at least according to current, widely prevalent belief, with a degree of 'naturalness.' The sports watching audience is interested in athletic performance, not biochemistry."[52]

In the current sporting climate, given the widespread efforts to keep steroids and similar substances out of the bodies of athletes, the officials who oversee the professional and collegiate leagues in America are not of a mind to legalize performance-enhancing drugs. Likewise, international sports officials are also opposed to the notion that steroids, human growth hormone, and blood doping should be made legal and administered to athletes under the supervision of physicians. In the future, athletes who use drugs to make themselves stronger and faster will likely continue to be regarded by most fans and fellow competitors in violation of the fundamental spirit that guides all sports—the spirit of fair play.

Facts

- A 2011 poll by the website YouGov.com reported that 56 percent of respondents are opposed to using government law enforcement entities—including grand juries—to investigate performance-enhancing drug use by athletes.

- A poll conducted in 2011 by the website EliteFitness .com, which is popular among bodybuilders and weightlifters, reported that 42 percent of respondents felt steroids should be legal and sold without a prescription.

- A 2010 online poll by the British newspaper *Guardian* found 58 percent of readers believe Lance Armstrong won his seven Tour de France victories with the help of performance-enhancing drugs.

- A 2011 poll sponsored by CBS News and *Vanity Fair* magazine found that 72 percent of respondents do not believe performance-enhancing drugs should be permitted in sports, even if the substances are regulated by the US Food and Drug Administration.

- After returning to the big leagues in 2011 following stem cell therapy, Bartolo Colon posted respectable statistics: He pitched 164 innings, his most since 2005; compiled an earned run average of 4.00, and started 26 games.

CHAPTER FOUR

Does Drug Testing Work?

Diana Taurasi may be one of the biggest stars in the Women's NBA, but her salary as a player for the Phoenix Mercury does not come close to the multimillion-dollar contracts offered to the male athletes who compete in the NBA. So during the WNBA's off-season, Taurasi earns extra paychecks by playing for a team in Turkey, where basketball is an enormously popular sport.

Late in 2010, as the Turkish women's basketball season was under way, Taurasi was notified by her team that she failed a drug test. According to the lab, Taurasi's urine tested positive for the drug modafinil, which is a stimulant. During her test, Taurasi provided two samples of urine, and in each sample traces of modafinil had been discovered. Taurasi denied taking the drug, but team officials felt they had no choice but to cut her from the team and rescind her contract.

Taurasi returned to America, knowing full well that a positive drug test could have a devastating effect on her career—making her ineligible for the WNBA as well as the 2012 Olympics. Moreover, Taurasi feared that despite all her accomplishments in women's basketball—including two Olympic gold medals and an MVP award from the WNBA—she would always have to live under the stigma that she cheated by taking a performance-enhancing drug. "It could not only ruin your career, but your reputation," Taurasi says. "I've . . . worked tremendously hard on the basketball court to be where I'm at. For this to be put on me was unfair."[53]

A few weeks after she arrived home from Turkey, Taurasi received some unexpected news: The Turkish lab that conducted Taurasi's urinalysis found errors in its testing procedures. The lab cleared Taurasi of using performance-enhancing drugs. "I got the news . . . at 5 a.m. and was in shock," Taurasi says. "It's really good that the facts came out and the truth came out."[54]

False Positives

Taurasi was the victim of a "false positive"—an error that incorrectly shows evidence of drug use in a sample. The lab that conducted the Taurasi test was the Turkish Doping Control Center at Hacettepe University in Ankara, Turkey, which had been accredited by the WADA to perform drug tests. After the lab admitted its mistake, Ugur Erdener, dean of the university, said it is likely the technicians misread the data.

Moreover, after the lab disclosed its error in the Taurasi case, the facility said it found mistakes in the tests administered to two soccer players; they were also exonerated and reinstated by their leagues. Says Turgay Demirel, president of the Turkish Basketball Federation, "It is very sad for our country that an institution accredited [by the] WADA committed such a huge mistake . . . Turkey, Turkish sports and Turkish basketball could pay a fairly high price for this."[55]

Demirel added that his league plans to find a new lab to conduct its drug tests. Overall, there are 35 labs worldwide that have been accredited by the WADA to conduct drug tests.

> "It is very sad for our country that an institution accredited [by the] WADA committed such a huge mistake . . . Turkey, Turkish sports and Turkish basketball could pay a fairly high price for this."[55]
>
> — Turgay Demirel, president of the Turkish Basketball Federation.

Tiny Snafus Hurt Reputations

Taurasi was cleared after a lab admitted it had erred in conducting the scientific chores involved in a drug test. But even tiny snafus in testing procedures can cast doubts over a player's reputation. During the 2011 pro football season, two members of the Dallas Cowboys faced possible suspensions because they had allegedly failed to show up for their drug tests just before the start of the season. Dez Bryant and DeMarco Murray both maintained they had taken the tests. After investigating the two cases, league officials exonerated both players, finding that they had taken the tests but neglected to give the technician their driver's licenses at the time of

Phoenix Mercury guard Diana Taurasi (in blue) was horrified to learn that she had failed a drug test in 2010. The lab that conducted the test later admitted to errors in their procedures and cleared her record but testing snafus remain a concern in all sports.

the tests. Therefore, Bryant and Murray were both marked absent when Cowboys team members were tested.

French cyclist Jeannie Longo also faced a suspension because of a technical error made by the French Cycling Federation. One of France's most popular athletes, Longo has been riding competitively since the 1984 Olympics. Fifty-three years old in 2011, Longo was still competing in cycling events against opponents half her age and hoped to qualify for the 2012 French Olympic team.

Longo had never tested positive for performance-enhancing

drugs but in 2011 she learned that she was under suspicion for breaking the French Cycling Federation's anti-doping rules. Under the rules, French cyclists are selected from time to time for membership in year-long drug-testing pools. While they are members of the pools, the athletes are required to advise the federation of their whereabouts so they can be administered random tests. Longo was told she had failed to keep the federation informed of her whereabouts and could face a career-ending suspension.

Did Longo deliberately keep the organization in the dark because she was juicing and knew she would fail a random test? After federation officials looked further into the case, they concluded that Longo's time in the pool had expired, and she was no longer obligated to keep the federation informed of her whereabouts. "We're very happy," says Longo's lawyer, Bruno Caraz. "It's a decision that does justice to Jeannie Longo."[56]

Chemical Analyses

The cases against Longo, Bryant, and Murray amounted to little more than paperwork errors while Taurasi's case reflected a significant breakdown in the science of drug testing. In actuality, false positives are known to be rare in drug testing, which is conducted through chemical analyses. Most drug tests are performed on samples of urine, but blood, saliva, and hair can also be analyzed.

During the course of the test, most league rules require the player to provide the sample in full view of the technician—in other words, the technician must observe the entire stream of urine as it leaves the athlete's body and enters the jar. Sports leagues insist on this requirement out of fear that if the athlete is permitted to provide the sample behind the closed door of a bathroom stall, the athlete would have an opportunity to substitute a clean sample furnished by somebody else.

Once the sample arrives back at the lab, the two techniques most labs employ to conduct the tests are gas chromatography and mass spectrometry. In gas chromatography, the sample is heated to a vapor and exposed to a gas, usually helium or nitrogen. These gases absorb molecules from the vaporized sample. The gas is then run through a glass column in what is known as the mobile phase.

The column is coated with a substance that absorbs the molecules from the sample. This is known as the retention phase. Eventually, the molecules from the sample will loosen themselves from the glass wall and leave the cylinder. It is the rate at which the molecules leave the cylinder that is measured. The molecules found in a specific anabolic steroid, for example, all have the same retention times. If the retention time for a specific test matches the

Drug Testing in America

The World Anti-Doping Agency has accredited 35 labs to conduct drug tests on athletes. Two of those labs are located in America: The University of Utah's Sports Medicine Research and Testing Laboratory in Salt Lake City, Utah, and the Olympic Analytical Laboratory at the University of California at Los Angeles (UCLA).

The UCLA lab tests more than 45,000 urine samples a year. Clients of the lab include the National Football League (NFL), National Collegiate Athletic Association (NCAA), and several baseball minor leagues. The Utah lab has also performed tests for the NFL and NCAA as well as the US Olympic Committee. The Utah lab has also tested high school athletes.

The UCLA lab was established with a grant in 1984 from the Los Angeles Olympic Organizing Committee, which staged the Summer Olympics that year in the California city. Later, the lab helped expose the BALCO scandal. The lab's founder, Donald Catlin, says he looks forward to the day when there are no performance-enhancing drugs in sports. He says, "My hope is, and I think it's not unrealistic, that you should be able to watch a track and field final and be satisfied that nobody is doping."

Quoted in Tom Goldman, "Anti-Doping Doctor Leaves California Lab," NPR, March 30, 2007. www.npr.org.

known retention time for the steroid, the test is considered positive for that steroid.

In mass spectrometry, the urine is bombarded with electrons that break down the sample into fragments made up of their component chemicals. The fragments then pass through a magnetic field that enables the technician to measure the mass of each fragment. The mass of each fragment is then compared to the masses of known performance-enhancing drugs. If the technician discovers a match, the test is regarded as positive.

The first lab whose sole mission was to test for performance-enhancing drugs was established in 1983 by Manfred Donike, a German chemist and former cyclist who developed the first tests for steroids. Donike set up a lab at the Pan American Games in Caracas, Venezuela, using gas chromatography and mass spectrometry. Donike's tests revealed that 19 athletes were taking anabolic steroids. Moreover, as the test results were announced, numerous athletes dropped out of the competition and returned home before Donike had a chance to test them—a certain indication those athletes had something to hide.

"Is it possible to tamper with the sample containers? Not without leaving evidence of it."[58]

— Caroline K. Hatton, former associate director of testing at the University of California at Los Angeles Olympic Analytical Laboratory.

Highest Levels of Accuracy

The gas chromatography and mass spectrometry tests are defended by labs and others, who insist that they are performed at the highest level of accuracy. A 2007 study authored by Caroline K. Hatton, former associate director of a testing laboratory at the University of California at Los Angeles, vouched for the accuracy of the tests and insisted that most labs follow strict guidelines established by the WADA as well as the individual professional and college leagues. She says, "A substantial international regulatory framework is in place to harmonize sports rules and drug-testing laboratories."[57]

One of those rules requires the samples to be kept in tamper-proof containers. "Is it possible to tamper with the sample containers? Not without leaving evidence of it," Hatton said. "Sample integrity is checked and documented upon receipt at the laboratory by technicians who inspect containers and tamper-evident seals visually. . . . The bottles used at the Olympics are sealed with a thick plastic cap over the stopper, and the only way to access the sample is to destroy the cap."[58]

Nevertheless, Hatton concludes, drug testing laboratories are constantly challenged to stay one step ahead of athletes, trainers, chemists, and physicians who continue to find new ways to mask the use of performance-enhancing drugs. She says, "Will anti-doping science ever get ahead of the cheats? . . . Crooked scientists can market new designer drugs overnight with no concern for FDA approval, and some athletes pay good money to be the ones to discover safety and efficacy or the lack thereof. Meanwhile, anti-doping scientists need months or years to develop and validate new tests."[59]

Testing Clean

Hatton's belief that athletes are constantly finding ways to fool the testing labs is supported by a long history of chicanery on the part of the athletes. Over the years, athletes have resorted to all manner of ruses to ensure their urine would test clean. Before the leagues adopted their present get-tough policies that require the athletes to provide the samples in full view of the technicians, many athletes found ways to buy urine on the Internet or convinced friends who do not use drugs to provide them with samples. For these athletes, it was a simple matter to transfer a friend's urine to the vial handed to them by the technicians, since the technicians had granted them the privacy of producing the samples behind the locked doors of bathroom stalls. Athletes were also known to drink large quantities of water to dilute the drug content, knowing that tests often miss trace amounts of drugs. Before diuretics were added to the list of banned drugs, they were consumed by athletes to promote urination as a way of purifying their samples. Some athletes used vitamin B3, also known as niacin, which is known to have a diuretic effect. Niacin was a popular choice because it is a legal substance available in supermarkets and pharmacies without a prescription. Athletes also added salt, bleach, and other substances to their urine to mask the drug content.

In the BALCO case, chemist Patrick Arnold pleaded guilty in 2009 to synthesizing an anabolic steroid capable of evading detection. Arnold created the drug by obtaining the results of gas chromatography and mass spectrometry tests on the steroid tetra-hydrogestrinone (THG). He then tweaked the ingredients of the steroid so they would not match the data on file about the drug. Arnold nicknamed the concoction "the clear" because it could not be detected by the tests. Arnold was eventually convicted on the charge of illegally distributing steroids and sentenced to three months in prison. Meanwhile, once the labs had access to Arnold's formula for THG, they were able to develop tests to detect it.

The Case of Onterrio Smith

Finding a way to fool the test rose to a level of absurdity with the case of Onterrio Smith, who played running back for the Minnesota Vikings. From his earliest days as a player, Smith showed enormous potential. At Grant High School in Sacramento, California, he set a school record by rushing for more than 3,100 yards (2,834 m) and scoring more than 60 touchdowns during the course of his career. By the time he enrolled at the University of Tennessee in 1999, he had already attracted the attention of pro scouts who admired his dogged tenacity and quick-burst ability.

But around campus in Knoxville, Smith's drug use had become no secret. In 2000 he was kicked off the University of Tennessee football team when he tested positive for marijuana. He transferred to the University of Oregon where he completed his college career. Smith should have been a first-round choice in the 2003 NFL draft, which would have guaranteed him a lucrative contract, but by then the pro teams were well aware of his history as a drug user and wary of paying the type of big money to him that is typically awarded to first-round choices. So Smith had to wait until the fourth round to be selected by the Vikings and, later, forced to sign a contract guaranteeing him a modest pro salary. Still, given his talents, Smith could have blossomed

"Hitters are older—and stronger—than they were years ago. It's impossible to measure the actual effect of performance enhancers, but it seems probable that they helped account for recent extremes in offensive achievement."[63]

— Fox Sports analyst Ken Rosenthal.

into a major star but over the course of his career with the Vikings Smith continued using drugs—both for recreational and performance-enhancing purposes. In 2004, while playing for the Vikings, he tested positive for steroids and was forced to sit out a four-game unpaid suspension.

In April 2006 Smith was detained at Minneapolis–St. Paul International Airport after a routine search of his luggage turned up several vials of white powder as well as a device known as the "Whizzinator." Despite its humorous name, use of the Whizzinator is no laughing matter. The device is used to fool drug tests. Smith had been detained at the airport because police believed the white powder found in his luggage was cocaine. In actuality, the powder was not cocaine but urine dried to a powdered state. By adding water and the powdered urine to the Whizzinator, the device is capable of delivering a drug-free urine sample.

Since owning a Whizzinator and powdered urine is not a violation of the law, Smith was not charged with a crime. However, the NFL took an interest in the case. League officials believed that Smith intended to use the Whizzinator to help him pass a drug test. The NFL came down hard on Smith, suspending him for a year. Says Greg Aiello, a spokesman for the NFL, "Under the terms of our policy, a deliberate attempt to substitute or alter a specimen during collection is a violation."[60] Smith never played pro football again. Following his suspension, the Vikings cut the running back, ending his pro football career after a mere three seasons in the league.

Better Home Run Hitters

Despite their success in catching athletes who try to mask the drug content of their urine, many sports officials and others contend the tests continue to be faulty—missing many drug users while accusing innocent people of using drugs. Daniel M. Rosen, author of the book *Dope: A History of Performance Enhancement in Sports from the Nineteenth Century to Today*, maintains that sports leagues have put too much trust in the work of the labs they hire to conduct their tests and that few tests are examined for their accuracy. "Lab testing is a curious thing," says Rosen. "One of the things we

Advance Warning in the NFL

The NFL insists that it employs one of the toughest drug testing procedures in professional sports, but in 2011 an incident in the locker room of the Green Bay Packers suggested that players were receiving advance warning of the tests. After a game, reporters observed the team's head trainer Pepper Burruss circulating among several players, advising them that they were to meet with him the following day. After Burruss spoke with lineman Scott Wells, the player turned to a reporter and said, "Drug test."

According to test experts, giving players a day's notice enables them to take steps to rid their bodies of banned substances. "If you are going to do advanced warning, you might as well not test," says David Howman, director general of the World Anti-Doping Agency.

In the Olympics as well as most other sports, when athletes are approached by sample collectors, they must provide the samples immediately and in full view of the collectors.

The NFL defended the policy of advance warning and said it is given in limited cases only. The day after a game is typically an off-day for players, a league official said, and giving players advance warning is intended to ensure they show up for the tests. Still, experts believe there should be no advance warning under any circumstances. Says Donald Catlin, founder of the Olympic Analytical Laboratory at the University of California at Los Angeles, "If you don't have surprise testing, [athletes] can run rings around you."

Quoted in Reed Albergotti, "Is the NFL Telegraphing Drug Tests?," *Wall Street Journal*, January 20, 2011. http://online.wsj.com.

need to know about it is that no test is perfect. Just because the A and the B samples actually give the same result doesn't necessarily mean that the result is correct. There are these funny things called false positives."[61] And Charles E. Yesalis, the Penn State professor of health and human development, believes faulty tests are a lot more common than the labs are likely to admit. "Drug tests catch only stupid, careless and foolish people,"[62] he says.

Experts are certain that athletes are either still finding ways to beat drug tests or that the testing procedures are faulty. Fox Sports analyst Ken Rosenthal points out that today's Major League baseball players are better home run hitters than the players of a generation ago. In 1975, Rosenthal says, the average player hit a home run in 2 percent of his plate appearances. Today's hitters slug home runs in 3 percent of their plate appearances. Moreover, they have managed to become better sluggers even though they are facing better pitching—the average speed of the fastball since 1975 has increased from 90 to 93 miles per hour. In addition, hitters have managed to hit more home runs against better pitching even though the average age of a Major League player has risen by more than two years. Today, the average age of a player is 29.2; back in 1975, the average age was 27.5. "Hitters are older—and stronger—than they were years ago," he says. "It's impossible to measure the actual effect of performance enhancers, but it seems probable that they helped account for recent extremes in offensive achievement."[63]

"The effectiveness of the global fight against doping depends on the ability of anti-doping laboratories to reliably identify . . . the substances prohibited in sport."[66]

— World Anti-Doping Agency.

Testing for HGH

Players have managed to improve their performances in an era in which drug testing has become more widely administered to athletes as well as more refined—more able to detect more varieties of drugs. For example, in 2011 the NFL announced it would start testing for human growth hormone even though for years testing for HGH has proven to be an inexact science. The NFL plans to use the standards for HGH adopted by the World Anti-Doping Agency, but leaders of the National Football League Players Association (NFLPA), the union that represents pro football players, insist those standards should not apply to its members. HGH is a hormone that can be found naturally in everyone's bodies. Since NFL players are among the largest athletes in the world, their

The NFL Players Association head DeMaurice Smith and other officials of the union contend that tests for human growth hormone are inexact and undependable. Football players, who are likely to have naturally higher levels of the hormone because of their size, could suffer from tests that fail to take size and other physical characteristics into account.

natural levels of HGH are likely to be higher than typical levels found in other athletes, such as female gymnasts or skaters. "What is the normal level of HGH?" asks George Atallah, an official of the NFLPA. "How does a woman swimmer from Eastern Europe compare with (New England Patriots nose tackle) Vince Wilfork."[64]

League officials counter that testing methods have improved and have cut down on the number of players who have used steroids. They point out that each year, the tests unveil drug use by athletes. In 2011, for example, New York Giants defensive tackle Jimmy Kennedy and Washington Redskins players Fred Davis and Trent Williams were suspended for four games after their tests came back positive for performance-enhancing drugs.

Long Ordeals

In some cases, players have refused to accept the results of their drug tests and have launched appeals in efforts to clear their names. In 2008 Minnesota Vikings players Kevin Williams and Pat Williams (they are unrelated) both tested positive for bumetanide, a banned diuretic that is regarded as a masking agent for anabolic steroids. The two players contended that the diuretic is contained in a nutritional supplement known as StarCaps that is not on the NFL's list of banned substances. The two players sued the NFL, contending that they had not intentionally taken a banned substance. In the meantime, the players were permitted to remain with the team.

After a legal process that took three years, a judge in Minnesota upheld the suspensions in 2011. By then, Pat Williams was 39 years old and had retired from professional football. Kevin Williams had the option of appealing to a higher court, but he had already spent $1 million in legal fees and agreed to accept the judge's order. He elected to serve his four-game unpaid suspension in 2011 and get on with his career. "We went through it for three years," Williams said after serving his suspension and rejoining his team. "The case is done. The suspension is done. The fine is done. It's officially over. Paid or not, I've been playing hard. I'm going to keep playing hard. I just want to win a game."[65]

Kevin Williams spent $1 million trying to prove his innocence. Meanwhile, Taurasi was falsely accused of an act that could have cost one of the world's top female basketball players her athletic career. Officials of sports leagues believe cases like Taurasi's are rare, though, and in the vast majority of cases the tests have correctly identified the users of performance-enhancing drugs. "The effectiveness of the global fight against doping depends on the ability of anti-doping laboratories to reliably identify . . . the substances prohibited in sport,"[66] says a statement issued by the

WADA. Those athletes who have been caught by laboratory analyses using performance-enhancing drugs could certainly vouch for the effectiveness of the tests, but for athletes like Taurasi, those words may hardly seem reassuring.

Facts

- Laboratories accredited by the World Anti-Doping Agency reported 1,266 positive drug samples in 2010. The labs provided tests for nearly 100 sports leagues and national anti-doping agencies. Overall, the labs tested 258,267 samples in 2010.

- Drug testing has become so sophisticated that most labs are now able to test for residue from microscopic particles of plastic released by the intravenous bags used by blood dopers. Alberto Contador, winner of the 2010 Tour de France, was stripped of his victory on evidence consisting in part of plastic particles found in his urine.

- Under the NFL's drug testing policy, every player is tested in training camp. After the season begins, the tests are conducted every week with 10 players from each team chosen randomly to provide urine samples. Players who have tested positive and reinstated after their suspensions are tested 24 times each season.

- The first American athlete suspended for using human growth hormone is Mike Jacobs, an infielder for the minor league Colorado Springs Sky Sox. After testing positive for HGH in 2010, Jacobs was forced to serve a 50-game suspension; following the suspension, he was cut from the team.

Are Dietary Supplements an Alternative to Performance-Enhancing Drugs?

Nonito Donaire is one of the world's top professional boxers. By 2012 his record stood at 27 wins, including 18 by knockout, and one loss. Thanks to his bulldog tenacity and a devastating left hook, he earned the World Boxing Council's championship in the bantamweight division, a class for boxers who weigh between 115 and 118 pounds (between 52 and 53.5 kg). According to *Ring* magazine, the bible of the sport of boxing, Donaire is—pound for pound—one of the top boxers in the world.

Donaire says he owes much of his success to Victor Conte—the former head of BALCO. After serving his prison term for supplying steroids to professional athletes, Conte went into a new business. His new company, Scientific Nutrition for Advanced Conditioning, now manufactures energy drinks that are packed with vitamins and nutritional supplements. Donaire is a dedicated customer. "Man, I have so much energy," Donaire told a reporter in 2011. "I feel amazing, I feel incredible."[67]

The name of Conte's energy drink is "PED," which Conte admits is something of an inside joke. PED are the initials for "performance-enhancing drugs," but in this case the initials stand for "performance energy drink." The drink that Donaire consumes contains ubiquinol, which is also known as coenzyme Q10, a substance manufactured naturally by the body that enhances blood flow through the arteries. PED also contains beta-alanine, a naturally occurring amino acid that helps build muscle mass; and L-carnitine, also a naturally occurring amino acid that increases red blood cell count. Finally, the drink contains L-arginine, an amino acid that enlarges blood vessels, thus aiding in blood circulation.

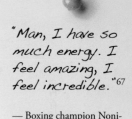

"Man, I have so much energy. I feel amazing, I feel incredible."[67]

— Boxing champion Nonito Donaire, a dedicated consumer of the energy drink PED.

All of these ingredients have the potential for improving athletic performance because they help deliver more red blood cells and, therefore, more oxygen, to the muscles. Donaire says he met with Conte before becoming a consumer of PED, and is convinced the drink has enhanced his strength and endurance. "He's helped me become a better fighter and athlete," Donaire says. "My performance level has increased dramatically."[68]

While it would seem that any professional athlete should be wary of developing a relationship with a convicted steroid peddler, Donaire insists that he checked out Conte and believes the former BALCO head has reformed and runs a legitimate business. Moreover, Donaire says, he is tested for performance-enhancing drugs before each fight and has never been found to be juicing. "This guy knows a lot," Donaire says of Conte. "Victor is like a father to me. We have a trust with each other."[69]

A $61 Billion Business

Donaire's dedication to an energy drink illustrates the popularity of nutritional supplements, which are also known as dietary supplements. Supplements are popular among athletes but other people consume them as well. According to the Natural Products

Filipino champion Nonito Donaire (left) is a devoted user of an energy drink that is filled with vitamins and nutritional supplements. Energy drinks and other nutritional supplements have become hugely popular among professional and recreational athletes.

Association, a supplements industry trade group, Americans spend $61 billion a year on nutritional supplements.

Athletes make up a large base of consumers who use nutritional supplements—they consume them for burning fat, building muscle, and producing energy and endurance. Supplements are available in pill form, as powders, or in liquid form. Many can be purchased on supermarket or pharmacy shelves, in stores that specialize in supplements, and through Internet-based distributors.

Magazines read by bodybuilders are packed with advertisements for supplements, practically cover to cover. Each ad proclaims that it will provide bodybuilders with muscle mass and energy as they work out. Moreover, many of these magazines feature stories by bodybuilders, trainers, and even physicians providing critiques and endorsements for supplements.

Under law, dietary supplements are subject to very little oversight by the US Food and Drug Administration (FDA). Under the US Dietary Supplement Health and Education Act of 1994, the onus for ensuring that supplements are safe falls on the manufacturers of the supplements. This means that consumers are generally on their own when they make decisions about using supplements, particularly when it comes to the quantities and frequencies of their dosages. If a supplement is found to be hazardous after it hits the market, the FDA can take action against the manufacturer. This action could include a ban on the manufacture, sale, and import of the supplement. Over the years, the FDA has taken action against several dietary supplements touted as weight-reducing aids. Perhaps the most notorious of these supplements is ephedra.

Death by Heat Stroke

Ephedra is an herb that grows in dry climates. It has been used for centuries as a home remedy for such ailments as colds, coughs, headaches, and even asthma. Ephedra is also used to help people lose weight because it constricts the blood vessels, which makes it more difficult for the body to release heat. As a result, the temperature of the body rises, which helps burn fat.

That is why Steve Bechler started taking ephedra. At 249 pounds (113 kg), the minor league pitcher was convinced that his girth was standing between him and a Major League contract. And so in 2003, when Bechler reported to spring training with the Baltimore Orioles, he went on a crash diet and also started consuming tablets composed of ephedra. On February 17, while working out with the Orioles, Bechler suddenly collapsed. At the hospital, Bechler's body temperature was found to be 108°F (42°C)—nearly 10°F (6°C) above normal. He died shortly after arriving in the emergency room. The cause of death was heat stroke—his body's high temperature caused his vital organs to shut down. "This was certainly a preventable death," says Joshua Perper, the pathologist who performed the autopsy on Bechler's body. "It didn't have to occur, this type of tragedy."[70]

After Bechler's death, the FDA issued a partial ban on the sale

"This was certainly a preventable death. It didn't have to occur, this type of tragedy."[70]

— Joshua Perper, the pathologist who performed the autopsy on pitcher Steve Bechler, who died after consuming ephedra.

of ephedra in America—the agency still permits acupuncturists to dispense the herb to their patients. Meanwhile, several professional and college leagues, including Major League Baseball, the International Olympic Committee, the National Football League, and the National Collegiate Athletic Association, added ephedra to their lists of banned substances.

Leaders in the supplements industry contend that the FDA and the sports leagues overreacted to the Bechler case. They insist that Bechler abused the substance. When ephedra is used in moderation, supplements experts believe it can be an effective and safe substance to help users lose weight. "[Bechler] was a fat guy exercising in the heat,"[71] insists Jack Owoc, chief executive officer of the supplements manufacturer Vital Pharmaceutics.

Owoc's belief that Bechler's lack of conditioning was mostly responsible for his death does not account for the case of Kory Stringer, a well-conditioned lineman for the Minnesota Vikings who collapsed on his team's practice field in 2001. On the morning of the July 31 practice, before taking the field, Stringer in-

Ephedra (pictured here in raw form) was implicated in the death of Steve Bechler of the Baltimore Orioles. After Bechler's death, the FDA issued a partial ban on the sale of ephedra in the United States and several sports leagues added it to their lists of banned substances.

gested capsules of Ripped Fuel, a dietary supplement containing ephedra. Under the blazing July sun, Stringer suffered heat stroke and died. Following Stringer's death, the NFL banned the use of ephedra by players.

Banned Substances

The Bechler and Stringer cases may have sparked a national discussion about ephedra, but in the years since their deaths the supplements industry has continued to grow. Hundreds of manufacturers and retailers have sprouted up, eager to cash in on the public's thirst for nutritional supplements. Rene Gonzalez opened his supplements store in Cape Coral, Florida, in 2008. Named "Just Add Muscle," the store caters to bodybuilders and other athletes. Gonzalez has no professional training in chemistry or nutrition—before going into the supplements business, he served in the US Marines and then found a job customizing cars. According to Gonzalez, he learned all he needs to know about supplements by taking them himself and reading about them in magazines and online. "Opening the store is the first step," Gonzalez says. "What I really hope to do is open my own manufacturing company. That's my dream: to franchise this store and manufacture my own supplements and then sell them in stores."[72]

> "It can take many years before we realize the effect of excessive doses of any supplement on our health."[76]
>
> — Exercise physiologist David Lightsey.

With so little oversight regulating the supplements industry, critics contend that just about anything—including steroids—can end up in a pill, drink, or powder sold over the counter in a supplements store. Football players Kevin Williams and Pat Williams learned that lesson when they tested positive for bumetanide, a banned diuretic that is an ingredient of a nutritional supplement they were taking.

Another professional athlete who learned he had been ingesting a banned substance was J.C. Romero, a pitcher for the Philadelphia Phillies who won two World Series games in 2008. Romero had been taking 6-OXO Extreme, an over-the-counter supplement marketed as a testosterone booster. But Romero was forced to serve a 50-game suspension in 2009 after he tested positive for androstenedione—an ingredient of 6-OXO Extreme. The chemical is the same steroid Mark McGwire has admitted using. In fact, a 2007 study by the Lexington, Kentucky–based screening laboratory Informed Choice found substances banned by the World Anti-Doping Agency in 25 percent of the 58 supplements it tested.

The Market for Creatine

In addition to using andro, McGwire has also acknowledged using creatine. McGwire's slugging competitor Sammy Sosa also said he used creatine during his career. Unlike andro, creatine is a nutritional supplement and is available over the counter. Creatine is regarded as one of the most popular supplements on the market. Creatine is an amino acid produced by the liver and stored in the muscles. People also absorb creatine from the meat and fish they eat. Research has shown creatine helps muscles release energy. This is an important function for an NFL lineman who has to block a 300-pound opponent (136 kg) at the snap of the ball, or a sprinter in need of a burst of energy to explode out of the blocks, or a weightlifter who intends to hoist barbells weighing hundreds of pounds over his or her head in the span of a few seconds. According to exercise physiologist Jim Stoppani, "[It's] the ultimate energy source for muscles."[73]

Several scientific studies have looked at creatine use, and researchers have concluded the supplement causes no adverse effects. "Oral creatine supplementation has become very popular among competitive athletes and recreational fitness enthusiasts," an Italian study concluded in 2004. "In this connection several Olympic athletes have ingested creatine supplementation for months and even years without reported side effects."[74]

But just because a supplement like creatine may be safe to consume does not guarantee that it will be effective. Indeed, a considerable body of scientific evidence suggests most dietary supplements fail to provide athletes any help at all in toning their bodies. Exercise physiologist David Lightsey is particularly critical of creatine, which he says reduces the body's ability to expel fluids. In other words, creatine users may find themselves urinating less because the body retains more water. Lightsey says that after a few weeks on a creatine supplement, an athlete will step on a scale and notice he or she weighs more—an indication, to them, that they are building muscle mass. Lightsey argues that creatine consumers are drawing bogus conclusions—that the extra weight they see on the scale is not more muscle but more water retained in the body. "Many consumers misinterpret this water retention as muscle mass development due to the increase in body weight,"[75] he says.

In fact, Lightsey insists, creatine may have an adverse effect on muscle development. He says studies have shown that water retention breaks down muscle tissue. Moreover, Lightsey says there is a lack of scientific research that has studied the long-term effects

As Strong as . . . an Ant?

A tiny ant can carry an object, such as a speck of dirt or piece of leaf, many times its own size, and it can lift an object three times its own weight.

Nutritional supplements makers noticed this phenomenon and wondered whether this power could be transferred to humans. So supplements makers started adding ecdysterone, a hormone found in insects, to their products. "Could there be some correlation between insects' superior strength ratio and this compound?" wonders an article posted on Bodybuilder.com and described in a 2009 *Sports Illustrated* article. "What would the effects be on vertebrates such as mammals? If we have the proportionate strength of an ant, for example, we could easily pick up a car."

The only problem is ecdysterone has no effect on humans. The Salk Institute for Biological Studies in San Diego, California, tested the hormone and found it does not increase strength in people. "Studies in my lab have shown that [ecdysterone is] completely innocuous in mammals," says Ronald M. Evans, a professor at the Salk Institute.

Quoted in David Epstein and George Dohrmann, "What You Don't Know Might Kill You," *Sports Illustrated*, May 15, 2009, p. 54.

of creatine use. "What effects would abnormally large doses of creatine and related possible water retention have on the brain over time?" Lightsey asks. "These are only speculative questions, but remember it can take many years before we realize the effect of excessive doses of any supplement on our health."[76]

Packed with Caffeine

While the beneficial effects of creatine remain under debate, few experts will disagree with the notion that the one nutritional supplement guaranteed to provide the user with a burst of energy is caffeine. In recent years, a large assortment of energy drinks packed with caffeine have surfaced on the market. Among these drinks are Red Bull, EndoRush, Speed Stack, and Extreme Energy Shot.

The energizing effects of caffeine have been no secret for centuries. The Chinese discovered the energy-producing benefits of teas containing caffeine around 600 BC. The Mayans who lived in Central Mexico prior to the Spanish conquest of the 1500s discovered the energizing powers of chocolate, which contains caffeine. One well-known legend, first reported by Antoine Faustus Nairon, a seventeenth-century Italian scholar, tells of an Ethiopian goatherd named Kaldi who discovered the energy produced by caffeine when his animals refused to sleep after eating the leaves and berries of particular plants as they foraged in the mountains. The next morning, Kaldi led his animals back to the same foraging area and they immediately ran to the same plants. When Kaldi ate the berries, he felt a sudden rush of energy as well. The berries that Kaldi and his goats had eaten were from coffee plants.

Today, anybody who needs a cup of coffee in the morning to start the day knows about the energy-producing powers of caffeine. The typical cup of coffee contains between 75 and 100 milligrams of caffeine. In contrast, a can of Speed Stack contains 250 milligrams.

For many people, though, too much caffeine can lead to trouble. According to Sandra A. Fryhofer, professor of medicine at

"Energy drinks contain too much caffeine. This can cause anxiety, nervousness, sleep problems, elevated blood pressure, and heart palpitations."[77]

— Sandra A. Fryhofer, professor of medicine at Emory University in Atlanta, Georgia.

Emory University in Atlanta, Georgia, overdosing on caffeine can lead to adverse effects on the body. She says,

> Energy drinks contain too much caffeine. This can cause anxiety, nervousness, sleep problems, elevated blood pressure, and heart palpitations. Although healthy people can tolerate moderate amounts of caffeine, the content in energy drinks exceeds what could be considered moderate. Adverse health consequences of caffeine intoxication include seizures, mania, stroke, and even sudden death. Energy drink–related health consequences reported in . . . studies include liver damage, kidney and respiratory problems, seizures, and agitation, as well as heart rhythm disturbances, heart failure, [and] high blood pressure.[77]

Moreover, some studies have indicated that heavy doses of caffeine can at best provide quick bursts of energy—in other words, anywhere from five to 20 minutes after consuming a caffeine-

Caffeine, which comes from the coffee plant, is found in much higher amounts in many energy drinks than in a typical cup of coffee. Moderate amounts of these drinks can cause anxiety, sleep problems, and high blood pressure. Consumption of large amounts can lead to seizures and even sudden death.

packed energy drink, the effect has already worn off. "It doesn't appear that caffeine improves sprint performance,"[78] reported the journal *Coach & Athletic Director* in 2007.

Some professional sports teams have responded to those warnings. Even though energy drinks are not on baseball's list of banned substances, in 2011 the Houston Astros and Arizona Diamondbacks stopped making Red Bull and other energy drinks available to players in their clubhouses—much to the displeasure of the players who relied on the beverages. "What are they going to ban next? Coffee? Soft drinks? It's so bizarre,"[79] complains Diamondbacks relief pitcher J.J. Putz.

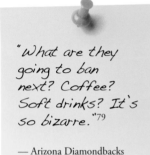

"What are they going to ban next? Coffee? Soft drinks? It's so bizarre."[79]

— Arizona Diamondbacks relief pitcher J.J. Putz.

Given the uncertainty of how nutritional supplements and energy drinks affect the body or athletic performance, many sports medicine experts counsel athletes to stick to the basics when it comes to training and preparing for competitions. According to Lightsey, a steady diet of carbohydrate-rich fruits, grains, and vegetables should provide most athletes with all the fuel they will need to stay competitive. Protein is also important for athletes because it builds and repairs muscles. Instead of swallowing protein supplements, Lightsey suggests nonfat powdered milk. Fats also provide energy. Lightsey recommends that athletes can consume the fats they need through nuts, raisins, and trail mix snacks. Hydration is also important—Lightsey recommends large doses of fluid—preferably water—before, during, and after exercising.

Succeeding at Any Cost

The use of nutritional supplements has exploded in an era when the sports leagues in America and elsewhere have cracked down on the use of steroids and other performance-enhancing drugs. Many athletes such as Donaire insist that dietary supplements provide them with extra strength and endurance. In fact, Donaire is convinced the supplements he receives by drinking PED are largely responsible for his status among the world's best boxers. Moreover, rather than consisting of chemical concoctions that make up steroids, human growth hormone and erythropoietin, the ingre-

Energy Drinks: More Than Just Caffeine

Energy drinks are packed with caffeine, but many also contain other supplements that can make them even more potent. Typical additives include guarana, a plant found in Brazil; green tea, a Chinese tea rich in disease-fighting antioxidants; yerba, a plant found in several South American countries; yohimbe, a plant imported from African countries; and bitter orange, a fruit found in Africa, Asia, and America.

According to the National Institutes of Health (NIH), these additives help give caffeine an extra kick. They can also increase the heart rate and raise blood pressure. The NIH says incidents in which athletes suffer ill effects from energy drinks are becoming common. In 2011 four high school football players in Orange County, California, were hospitalized with rapid heartbeats—a condition known as tachycardia. "All four had [consumed] super caffeinated drinks," says Michael F. Shepard, a physician and member of the California Interscholastic Federation Medical Advisory Board. "If you add dehydration or flu or muscle-building supplements like creatine to that, there can be an increased risk of fatal [irregular heartbeat]. These kids all did fine, but the heart is a muscle, too."

Quoted in Jorge Ortiz and Gary Graves, "Young Athletes, Energy Drinks," *USA Today*, December 2, 2011, p. 1A.

dients of nutritional supplements are all natural—distilled from plants or oils secreted by fish and other animals. On the other hand, the death of Bechler proves that just because a supplement is composed of a common herb like ephedra does not make it safe.

Certainly, while many athletes doubt the effectiveness of supplements, they still desire a competitive edge over their opponents. That is why in an era when drug testing has become a routine part of sports, each year brings new revelations about top-level athletes caught using steroids and other drugs. Charles E. Yesalis, the Penn State professor of health and human development, blames the culture of sports in America and elsewhere for the attitude harbored by athletes who are willing to juice to succeed. It is a culture that promises fame and fortune to the athlete who can run faster and throw harder than his or her opponents. He says these athletes learn at an early age that success in sports is the gateway to wealth and celebrity. He says,

> The sixth-grader knows what it takes to make the junior high team. The junior varsity player knows what it takes to make the varsity. The varsity player knows what it takes to make all-state and vie for a college scholarship. The freshman in college football knows what it takes to make the starting lineup sooner rather than later. The starter on the college team knows what it takes to possibly go on to a pro career.

> All this is driven—besides our desire to look good and be winners—because these drugs *work*, and many work well. . . . Anabolic steroids, in my strong professional opinion, will take athletes to heights they never would have attained naturally. The window of athletic opportunity is very small. You don't have five years to get an athletic scholarship. If you're not big enough your junior year in high school to play . . . college ball, there aren't going to be any miracles out there, to make gains naturally.[80]

It would seem, then, that Major League Baseball, the International Olympic Committee, the National Football League, and other major sports organizations have no choice but to continue their hard-nosed attitudes toward drug use by the athletes who play their games. It is an attitude they are forced to maintain, because many athletes have shown their desire to excel at any cost.

Facts

- Caffeine is most potent when consumed with carbohydrates, which can be found in whole grains, vegetables, fruits, and beans. A 2011 study by Sheffield Hallam University in Great Britain found that a drink composed of caffeine and carbohydrates helped soccer players improve their endurance and agility.

- A 2011 study commissioned by the International Olympic Committee found many supplements contain trace amounts of the steroid nandrolone. Although the amounts were small, the quantity found in the supplements is still high enough to be detected by a drug test.

- Many supplements contain arginine-alpha-ketoglutarate (AAKG), which is touted as a vasodilator—meaning it will open blood vessels and deliver more oxygen to muscles. A 2011 Baylor University study found that AAKG has, at best, a minimal ability to widen blood vessels.

- A 2011 study by North Carolina State University found that when mustard is fed to lab rats, it has an effect similar to steroids without the side effects. The researchers cautioned the tests were limited to lab rats and said people should not expect similar results.

- According to a 2011 Australian study, bodybuilding supplements that contain the amino acid L-tyrosine can significantly build up muscle in children who suffer from the muscle-wasting disease known as nemaline myopathy, which affects one in about 50,000 children.

- By 2012 the US Food and Drug Administration had banned 72 dietary supplements that were designed to help users lose weight but contained ingredients regarded as health hazards.

Source Notes

Introduction: The Steroid Era

1. Lisa Olson, "Maris' Record Has Aged Better than Most," *Sporting News*, October 10, 2011, p. 64.

2. Jose Canseco, *Juiced: Wild Times, Rampant 'Roids, Smash Hits, and How Baseball Got Big*. New York: HarperCollins, 2005, p. 9.

3. Quoted in Olson, "Maris' Record Has Aged Better than Most," p. 64.

4. Quoted in Daniel M. Rosen, *Dope: A History of Performance Enhancement in Sports from the Nineteenth Century to Today*. Westport, CT: Praeger, 2008, p. 39.

5. Quoted in Jorge Castillo, "Maris Honored at Yankee Stadium," *New York Times*, September 24, 2011. http://bats.blogs.nytimes.com.

Chapter One: What Is the Origin of the Drug Use Controversy in Sports?

6. Quoted in *Vancouver Sun*, "Georges Laraque Bio Attacks Steroid Use," November 7, 2011. www.vancouversun.com.

7. Quoted in *Vancouver Sun*, "Georges Laraque Bio Attacks Steroid Use."

8. Andrew J.M. Gregory and Robert W. Fitch, "Sports Medicine: Performance-Enhancing Drugs," *Pediatric Clinics of North America*, August 2007, p. 797.

9. Quoted in Sally Jenkins, "Winning, Cheating Have Ancient Roots," *Washington Post*, August 3, 2007. www.washingtonpost.com.

10. Quoted in Rosen, *Dope*, p. 33.

11. Jim Bouton, *Ball Four*. New York: Dell, 1970, p. 159.

12. Quoted in *New York Times*, "Bouton Is Warned by Kuhn on Content of His Writings," June 2, 1970, p. 47.

13. Quoted in Dermot McEvoy, "The Wrongs of Spring," *Publishers Weekly*, March 9, 2009, p. 20.

14. Dave Meggyesy, *Out of Their League*. Lincoln: University of Nebraska Press, 2005, p. 103.

15. Quoted in Sandy Padwe, "Drugs in Sports: Symptoms of a Deeper Malaise," *Nation*, September 27, 1986, p. 276.

16. Quoted in Rosen, *Dope*, p. 139.

17. Quoted in NBC Sports, "Jones Pleads Guilty, Admits Lying About Steroids," October 5, 2007. http://nbcsports.msnbc.com.

18. Quoted in Juliet Macur, "Bonds Guilty of Obstruction, but Not of Perjury," *New York Times*, April 14, 2011, p. A1.

19. Quoted in ESPN, "Mitchell Report: Baseball Slow to React to Steroid Use," December 13, 2007. http://sports.espn.go.com.

20. Quoted in ESPN, "Mitchell Report."

21. Quoted in Tom Haudicourt, "Ryan Braun Comes Out Swinging, Explains Innocence," JSOnline, February 24, 2012. www.jsonline.com.

22. Quoted in Don Walker, "Man Who Collected Sample Now at Center of Braun Controversy," *Milwaukee Journal Sentinel*, February 24, 2012. www.jsonline.com.

Chapter Two: How Do Performance-Enhancing Drugs Affect Athletes?

23. Quoted in Kevin Eck, "Revisiting a Life Spent on the Ropes: Superstar Billy Graham, Others to Appear at the Capitol Wrestling Legends Fanfest," *Baltimore Sun*, August 10, 2006.

24. Superstar Billy Graham and Keith Elliot Greenberg, *Tangled Ropes*. New York: Simon & Schuster, 2006, p. 165.

25. Quoted in ESPN, "Anabolic Steroids," September 6, 2007. http://espn.go.com.

26. Quoted in Steve Kettmann, "Girlz II Men," *New Republic*, July 3, 2000, p. 17.

27. Quoted in Steve Kettmann, "East German Olympic Dopers Guilty," *Wired*, July 18, 2000. www.wired.com.

28. Quoted in PBS, "Doping for Gold: The State-Sponsored Doping Program," *Secrets of the Dead*, June 13, 2011. www.pbs.org.

29. Quoted in PBS, "Doping for Gold."

30. Quoted in CNN, "Athlete Says Sports Steroids Changed Him from Woman to Man," August 11, 2008. http://articles.cnn.com.

31. Quoted in Rosen, *Dope*, p. 77.

32. Quoted in Rosen, *Dope*, p. 80.

33. Lyle Alzado, "I'm Sick and I'm Scared," *Sports Illustrated*, July 8, 1991, p. 20.

Chapter Three: Are Drug Users Cheaters?

34. Julian Savulescu, Bennett Foddy, and M. Clayton, "Why We Should Allow Performance-Enhancing Drugs in Sport," *British Journal of Sports Medicine*, December 2004, p. 667.

35. Savulescu, Foddy, and Clayton, "Why We Should Allow Performance-Enhancing Drugs in Sport," p. 667.

36. Savulescu, Foddy, and Clayton, "Why We Should Allow Performance-Enhancing Drugs in Sport," p. 667.

37. Thomas H. Murray, *From Birth to Death and Bench to Clinic*. Garrison, NY: Hastings Center, 2008, p. 154.

38. Matthew Herper, "The Case for Performance-Enhancing Drugs in Sport," *Forbes*, May 20, 2011. www.forbes.com.

39. Quoted in NBC Sports, "Goodell Confirms NFL Will Insist on HGH Testing," April 4, 2011. http://profootballtalk.nbc sports.com.

40. Quoted in Mel Antonen, "Poll: Baseball Fans Back Tougher Drug Policy," *USA Today*, December 1, 2004. www.usatoday.com.

41. Quoted in *USA Today*, "McCain: Baseball 'Can't Be Trusted,'" March 20, 2005. www.usatoday.com.

42. Christine Brennan, "Time for Selig to Strike Out Bonds' Marks," *USA Today*, April 21, 2011, p. 3C.

43. Quoted in David Callahan, *The Cheating Culture: Why More Americans Are Doing Wrong to Get Ahead*. New York: Harcourt, 2004, pp. 75–76.

44. Quoted in Selena Roberts and David Epstein, "The Case Against Lance Armstrong," *Sports Illustrated*, January 24, 2011, p. 56.

45. Quoted in *USA Today*, "Ex-Teammate Says Armstrong Used EPO," May 20, 2011, p. 9C.

46. Quoted in Reed Albergotti and Vanessa O'Connell, "Cyclist Armstrong Denies Doping," *Wall Street Journal*, May 20, 2010. http://online.wsj.com.

47. Greg Couch, "The Latest Accusations Against Armstrong Are Reason to Suspend Our Belief," *Sporting News*, June 6, 2011, p. 63.

48. Bill Strickland, "Endgame," *Bicycling*, May 2011, p. 48.

49. Quoted in Ian Austen, "2010 Tour de France Winner Found Guilty of Doping," *New York Times*, February 7, 2012, p. B13.

50. Howard Bryant, "Bartolo Colon Surgery: New Arms Race?," ESPN .com, May 25, 2011. http://sports.espn.go.com.

51. William Saletan, "The Beam in Your Eye: If Steroids Are Cheating, Why Isn't LASIK?," *Slate*, April 18, 2005. www.slate.com.

52. Urban Wiesing, "Should Performance-Enhancing Drugs in Sport Be Legalized Under Medical Supervision?," *Sports Medicine*, February 1, 2011, p. 173.

Chapter Four: Does Drug Testing Work?

53. Quoted in AOL News, "'False Positive' Vindicates Diana Taurasi," February 17, 2011. www.aolnews.com.

54. Quoted in John Altavilla, "Diana Taurasi Cleared," *Hartford Courant*, February 16, 2011. http://articles.courant.com.

55. Quoted in ESPN, "Diana Taurasi Test Lab Asked to Explain," February 17, 2011. http://sports.espn.go.com.

56. Quoted in Gregor Brown, "Longo Avoids Doping Suspension, Ricco Fined and Sentenced," *Cycling Weekly*, November 23, 2011. www.cyclingweekly.co.uk.

57. Caroline K. Hatton, "Beyond Sports Doping Headlines: The Science of Laboratory Tests for Performance-Enhancing Drugs," *Pediatric Clinics of North America*, August 2007, p. 716.

58. Hatton, "Beyond Sports Doping Headlines," p. 716.

59. Hatton, "Beyond Sports Doping Headlines," p. 731.

60. Quoted in *USA Today*, "Back's 'Whizzinator' Prompts NFL Inquiry," May 12, 2005, p. 1C.

61. Quoted in Anna North, "Could Diana Taurasi Be Exonerated for Doping?," Jezebel, January 31, 2011. http://jezebel.com.

62. Quoted in Dave Kindred, "It Doesn't Take a Genius to Pass a Steroids Test," *Sporting News*, August 19, 2002, p. 80.

63. Ken Rosenthal, "Even with Testing, Offenses Will Be Pumped Up," *Sporting News*, March 4, 2005, p. 56.

64. Quoted in Christian Red and Michael O'Keeffe, "NFL, Congressional Leaders Say League Will Start Screening for HGH, but Union Not Ready to Commit," *New York Daily News*, October 14, 2011. http://articles.nydailynews.com.

65. Quoted in Patrick Reusse, "No Money, No Fun So Far for Kevin Williams," *Minneapolis Star Tribune*, October 9, 2011. www.startribune.com.

66. World Anti-Doping Agency, "Accreditation Process," 2012. www.wada-ama.org.

Chapter Five: Are Dietary Supplements an Alternative to Performance-Enhancing Drugs?

67. Quoted in Geoffrey Gray, "78 Minutes with Victor Conte," *New York*, November 7, 2011, p. 20.

68. Quoted in Teri Thompson and Christian Red, "Business and Clients like Nonito Donaire Are Flocking Back to BALCO Founder Victor Conte," *New York Daily News*, September 17, 2011. http://articles.nydailynews.com.

69. Quoted in Thompson and Red, "Business and Clients like Nonito Donaire Are Flocking Back to BALCO Founder Victor Conte."

70. Quoted in Jarrett Murphy, "Ephedra Tied to Pitcher's Death," CBS News, February 17, 2003. www.cbsnews.com.

71. Quoted in David Epstein and George Dohrmann, "What You Don't Know Might Kill You," *Sports Illustrated*, May 15, 2009, p. 54.

72. Quoted in Epstein and Dohrmann, "What You Don't Know Might Kill You," p. 54.

73. Jim Stoppani, "The Encyclopedia of Supplements," *Flex*, December 2011, p. 201.

74. E. Bizzarini and L. DeAngelis, "Is the Use of Oral Creatine Safe?," *Journal of Sports Medicine and Physical Fitness*, December 2004, p. 414.

75. David Lightsey, *Muscles, Speed and Lies: What the Sport Supplement Industry Does Not Want Athletes or Consumers to Know*. Guilford, CT: Lyons, 2006, p. 125.

76. Lightsey, *Muscles, Speed and Lies*, p. 126.

77. Sandra A. Fryhofer, "Caffeinated Energy: Drinks with Dangers," Medscape, March 24, 2011. www.medscape.com.

78. Matt Brzycki, "Pills, Powders and Potions," *Coach & Athletic Director*, March 2007, p. 63.

79. Quoted in Christian Red, "No Red Bull in the Clubhouse as Astros and Diamondbacks Stop Providing Energy Drink to Players," *New York Daily News*, September 22, 2011. http://articles.nydailynews.com.

80. Quoted in Matt Chaney, *Spiral of Denial: Muscle Doping in American Football*. Warrensburg, MO: Four Walls, 2009, p. 6.

Related Organizations and Websites

Anti-Doping Research

3873 Grand View Blvd.
Los Angeles, CA 90066
phone: (310) 482-6925
e-mail: info@antidopingresearch.org
website: www.antidopingresearch.org

Anti-Doping Research is a nonprofit agency that researches new drugs that athletes may be using to enhance their abilities. By following the link to "Locker Room," visitors to the group's website can read comments by professional athletes on the dangers of performance-enhancing drugs.

Informed Choice

HFL Sport Science
1745 Alysheba Way, Suite 160
Lexington, KY 40509
website: www.informed-choice.org

Sponsored by the HFL Sport Science laboratory, this website enables consumers to enter the name of a dietary supplement and learn whether it has been tested for banned substances. By following the link for "Athletes and Coaches," visitors can download the publications *Sport Supplements: An Anti-Doping Backgrounder* and *Athlete's Guide to Nutrition*.

Mayo Clinic

200 First St. SW
Rochester, MN 55905
phone: (507) 284-2511
fax: (507) 284-0161
website: www.mayoclinic.com

The world-famous research hospital maintains a website providing extensive information about performance-enhancing drugs, explaining the risks of consuming anabolic steroids, human growth hormone, erythropoietin, and similar substances. Visitors can also follow links to information on energy drinks and nutritional supplements.

National Institute on Drug Abuse (NIDA)

6001 Executive Blvd., Room 5213
Bethesda, MD 20892
phone: (301) 443-1124
e-mail: information@nida.nih.gov
website: www.drugabuse.gov

An agency of the National Institutes of Health, NIDA supports scientific research into drugs that are commonly abused, including performance-enhancing drugs. By entering "steroids" or the names of other performance-enhancing drugs into the agency website search engine, students can find many resources on substances abused by athletes.

Natural Products Association

1773 T St. NW
Washington, DC 20009
phone: (800) 966-6632
fax: (202) 223-0250
e-mail: natural@NPAinfo.org
website: www.NPAinfo.org

This association of more than 1,900 retailers and manufacturers of supplements promotes the use of dietary supplements and supports research into their effects on consumers. Visitors to the association's website can follow the link to "Science Matters," where the safety of supplements and efforts by the government to regulate their use are addressed.

United States Anti-Doping Agency (USADA)

5555 Tech Center Dr., Suite 200
Colorado Springs, CO 80919
phone: (866) 601-2632
fax: (719) 785-2001
e-mail: media@usada.org
website: www.usada.org

Established in 2000, USADA oversees the drug tests administered to US Olympic athletes and supports scientific research into the effects of performance-enhancing drugs. Visitors to the USADA website can access issues of the agency's *Spirit of Sport* newsletter, which contains information on the USADA's anti-doping programs.

US Food and Drug Administration (FDA)

10903 New Hampshire Ave.
Silver Spring, MD 20993
phone: (888) 463-6332
website: www.fda.gov

The FDA monitors the nutritional supplements industry in America and can order products taken off the market if they prove to be hazardous to human health or contain performance-enhancing drugs. Its website provides an "Overview of Dietary Supplements," outlining what constitutes a dietary supplement and what information manufacturers must disclose to consumers.

US National Library of Medicine

Dietary Supplements Label Database
Two Democracy Plaza, Suites 440 and 510
6707 Democracy Blvd., MSC 5467
Bethesda, MD 20892
phone: (888) FIN-DNLM
fax: (301) 480-3537

e-mail: tehip@teh.nlm.nih.gov
website: http://dietarysupplements.nlm.nih.gov

An agency of the National Institutes of Health, the National Library of Medicine maintains a database of all dietary supplements available to American consumers. The library provides the list in alphabetical order; the ingredients, how the supplements work and known side effects for each supplement are listed. The database also includes a list of banned supplements.

Vanderbilt University Jean and Alexander Heard Library
419 21st Ave. South
Nashville, TN 37203
phone: (615) 322-7100
fax: (615) 343-8279
website: http://diglib.library.vanderbilt.edu

The library's website "Drugs in Sports: Issues and Groups" offers students several sources of information about performance-enhancing drugs, including the congressional testimony of Jose Canseco, Mark McGwire, and other steroid users; news articles about steroids in baseball; and reports by league officials detailing efforts to rid their sports of performance-enhancing drugs.

World Anti-Doping Agency (WADA)
Stock Exchange Tower
800 Place Victoria, Suite 1700
Montreal, QC H4Z 1B7
Canada
phone: (514) 904-9232
fax: (514) 904-8650
e-mail: info@wada-ama.org
website: www.wada-ama.org

WADA is the main international body that coordinates activities of some 600 international sports federations in combatting performance-enhancing drug use among athletes. Visitors to the WADA website can follow the link to "Prohibited List," which lists every substance outlawed by the agency.

Additional Reading

Books

Rob Beamish, *Steroids: A New Look at Performance-Enhancing Drugs*. Santa Barbara, CA: Praeger, 2011.

Mike Greenwood, Douglas Kalman, and Jose Antonio, eds., *Nutritional Supplements in Sports and Exercise*. Totowa, NJ: Humana, 2010.

Thomas M. Hunt, *Drug Games: The International Olympic Committee and the Politics of Doping, 1960–2008*. Austin: University of Texas Press, 2011.

David R. Mottram, ed., *Drugs in Sport*. New York: Routledge, 2011.

Jeffrey R. Stout, Jose Antonio, and Douglas Kalman, eds., *Essentials of Creatine in Sports and Health*. Totowa, NJ: Humana, 2010.

Andrew Tilin, *The Doper Next Door: My Strange and Scandalous Year on Performance-Enhancing Drugs*. Berkeley, CA: Counterpoint, 2011.

Periodicals

Jorge Ortiz and Gary Graves, "Young Athletes, Energy Drinks," *USA Today*, December 2, 2011.

Gregory Pratt, "Superstar Billy Graham Made It Big in Wrestling: Now the Steroids That Got Him There May Be Killing Him," *Phoenix New Times*, March 31, 2011.

Diane Pucin, "Mercury Star Diana Taurasi Bounces Back," *Los Angeles Times*, June 9, 2011.

Selena Roberts and Dana Epstein, "The Case Against Lance Armstrong," *Sports Illustrated*, January 24, 2011.

Bill Strickland, "Endgame," *Bicycling*, May 2011.

Internet Sources

ESPN, "Drugs and Sports." http://espn.go.com/special/s/drugsandsports.

PBS, "Doping for Gold: The State-Sponsored Doping Program," *Secrets of the Dead.* www.pbs.org/wnet/secrets/features/doping-for-gold/the-state-sponsored-doping-program/52.

ProCon.org, "Historical Timeline: History of Performance-Enhancing Drugs in Sports." http://sportsanddrugs.procon.org/view.resource.php?resourceID=002366.

USA Today, "BALCO Investigation Timeline." www.usatoday.com/sports/balco-timeline.htm.

Index

Note: Boldface page numbers indicate illustrations.

Kuhn, Bowie, 15

Landis, Floyd, 45–46, **46,** 47
lantern jaw, 33
Laraque, Georges, 10–11, **12**
L-arginine, 69
LASIK surgery, 43
L-carnitine, 69
Lightsey, David, 73, 74–76, 78
Linton, Arthur, 19
Longo, Jeannie, 56–57
Long Season, The (Brosnan), 16
Lorz, Fred, 42
L-tyrosine, 81

Major League Baseball (MLB), 6
  amphetamine use in, 14–15, 16
  investigation of steroid use in,
    19–20
  random drug testing initiated
    by, 8
  suspensions for performance-
    enhancing drug use in, 24, 44
Maris, Randy, 6, 8, 9
Maris, Roger, 6, **7**
Maris, Roger, Jr., 6, 8
mass spectrometry, 59
McCain, John, 42
McGwire, Mark, 6–7, 43,
  Hall of Fame and, 48
  records set by, 44
  use of androstenedione by, 28, 74
McNamee, Brian, 20
Meggyesy, Dave, 15–16
Men and Masculinities (journal), 24
Michael, Jimmy, 19
Mitchell, George, 19–20
modafinil, 54
Murray, DeMarco, 55
Murray, Thomas H., 39, 41
mustard, 81
Muto, Pasquale, 33

Nairon, Antoine Faustus, 76
nandrolone, 81
National Baseball Hall of Fame, 48
National Football League (NFL)
  advanced warning of drug testing
    in, 63

amphetamine use in, 15–16
drug testing policy of, 67
National Football League Players
  Association (NFLPA), 64–65
National Hockey League (NHL),
  10–11
National Institutes of Health
  (NIH), 79
Natural Products Association,
  69–70
nemaline myopathy, 81
niacin (vitamin B3), 60
nutritional supplements, 69–71,
  78–80
  banned substances in, 73–74

Olson, Lisa, 6
Olympic Games
  first drug testing in, 43–44
  steroid use by East German team
    in, 29–31
  use of drugs at first Games, 11
opinion polls. *See* surveys
Out of Their League (Meggyesy), 15

Palmeiro, Rafael, 48
performance-enhancing drugs
  calls for legalization of, 39–42
  historical use of, 11–13, 42–43
  incentives for use of, 23
  number of Major League players
    suspended for use of, 24
  See also specific drugs
Perper, Joshua, 71
Pettitte, Andy, 33
polls. *See* surveys
Positively False (Landis), 45–46
Putz, J.J., 78

Ricco, Ricardo, 33–34
Ring (magazine), 68
Rogge, Jacques, 18
roid rage, 8, 32
Romanowski, Bill, 17
Romero, J.C., 73–74
Rosen, Daniel, 62–63
Rosenthal, Ken, 61, 64
Ruth, Babe, 6